PLEASURES AND TREASURES

RARE STAMPS

ENDPAPERS: Great Britain: 1840 1d black, plate II

L. N. AND M. WILLIAMS

RARE STAMPS

G. P. PUTNAM'S SONS
NEW YORK

Acknowledgements

The authors and publishers wish to express their grateful thanks for the loan of illustrations and permission to reproduce them in this book to:

The Trustees of the British Museum
Deutsche Bundespost Museum
Thomas Allen
Bridger and Kay Ltd
Stanley Gibbons Ltd
H. R. Harmer Ltd
I. I. Ingraham

Robson Lowe Ltd
H. L. Katcher
Harmer, Rooke and Co. Ltd
Ernst Müller AG
Dr Achille Rivolta
Julius P. Steindler
Sir Henry Tucker

Figures 4, 16–21, 23, 24 are reproduced by gracious permission of Her Majesty the Queen

Bibliography

Stamps of Fame, L. N. and M. Williams (Blandford Press) 1949
The Postage Stamp Its History & Recognition, L. N. and M. Williams (Penguin Books) 1956
Stamps of Great Price, Nevile L. Stocken (A. E. Hopkins) 1932
Fabulous Stamps, John W. Nicklin, (Hastings House) 1939
Handbook of the Private Local Posts, E. F. Hurt & L. N. and M. Williams (F. Billig) 1950
Postage Stamps Worth Fortunes, Fred J. Melville (F. J. Melville) 1908
The Royal Philatelic Collection, Sir John Wilson, Bt (Dropmore Press) 1953
The Tapling Collection of Postage and Telegraph Stamps and Postal Stationery, James A. Mackay (Trustees of the British Museum) 1964

AUTHORS' NOTE: Many of the coloured illustrations would have reproduced unused or mint stamps; but, in order to comply with the requirements of 18 USC 504, as amended by Public Law 85 901, they appear used.

Contents

Foreword

This book illustrates some of the world's rarest stamps and relates their stories. Colourful meandering rather than arid studiousness has been the motive, and there is room for discussion about the exclusion of some issues in favour of others but there can be no gainsaying that, substantially, every stamp mentioned is recognized throughout the world of philately as a rarity.

Most of the stamps described are those that collectors call 'classics' – issued mainly, but not exclusively, before 1875, when the establishment of the Universal Postal Union and the increase of prepaid world wide correspondence necessitated the production of more examples of each issue.

Rarity and price, like fame and fortune, do not necessarily go hand in hand; we might contrast, by way of random example, the Canadian 'Twelve Pence Black' and the Gauthier Frères' steamship stamp.

Although the delights of meandering have been contrasted with the toils of study, it would be ungracious indeed of us to omit here to pay tribute to the students whose labours have established and recorded the truth of the claim that many valuable stamps can offer great pleasure.

1 Saxony: 1850 3pf red. Part of the sheet saved from the firescreen

CHAPTER ONE

The most famous rarities

2 Mauritius: 1847 (Post Office). The copper plate from which the issue was printed

EVERYBODY who has ever had some pretensions to collecting stamps has heard of the 'Post Office' Mauritius. The stamps, 1d red and 2d blue, were printed in the summer of 1847 from a small copper plate, engraved by James Barnard, a half-blind watchmaker and the only person on the island with a practical knowledge of engraving. The plate, which is still in existence, bears the two engravings side by side, and they were printed one at a time by inking each design separately.

Only 500 examples of each value were produced, so that they were by modern standards rarities from the start. Many of the stamps were used on invitations to a fancy-dress ball given at Government House, Port Louis, by Lady Gomm, wife of the Governor of Mauritius; indeed, it has been said that their issue was hurried for that use. Some were used on letters to France and India, but not one is known on a letter to England.

In all, twenty-six examples of the 'Post Office' Mauritius have been found (one in 1947, the stamps' centenary year), fourteen of the 1d, of which two are unused, and twelve of the 2d, of which four are unused.

A unique letter, bearing one stamp of each value, addressed to 'Messieurs Ducan & Lurgnie, Bordeaux' [figure 28], was discovered in 1902 by a French schoolboy while searching through that firm's correspondence, in the hope of

3 (*opposite*) Nova Scotia: 1851 1s violet

4 The 2d Post Office Mauritius in the Royal Collection

finding the stamps, about which he had read in a stamp magazine. There were many dusty correspondence files through which the boy had to search, and he had almost lost hope when he came across this remarkable letter and also another, bearing a 2d stamp alone. The boy's pertinacity was well rewarded when, early in 1903, he sold the two letters to a dealer in Paris for a total of £2,800. After passing through several famous collections, the unique letter came on the London auction market on 1 October 1963, and was sold by Robson Lowe Ltd, for £28,000. The purchaser was Raymond Weill, a dealer, of New Orleans.

Another extremely fine piece is an envelope bearing two specimens of the 1d and now in the collection of Mrs Louise Boyd Dale. The envelope, addressed to 'Thos. Jessom, Esq., Secretary of the Bombay Auxiliary Bible Society, The Esplanade, Bombay [figure 5], was bought for £50 in an Indian bazaar in 1897 by a man named Howard, who sold it the following year to a London dealer for £1,600; by 1906 the price had risen to £2,200; sixty years later it is difficult to place a price on this delectable rarity, but if it were to come on the market, the figure could scarcely be less than £50,000.

Undoubtedly, the finest individual stamp of this issue is the uncancelled 2d [figure 4], bought by the Prince of Wales, later King George v, in 1904 for £1,450. This example, with large margins, is now in the Royal Collection at Buckingham Palace.

The various hands through which the twenty-six examples of these rare stamps have passed have been traced by the present writers in another book (*Stamps of Fame*, Blandford Press, 1949).

Far rarer and more valuable than the 'Post Office' Mauritius is the stamp commonly referred to as 'the world's rarest'. This is the British Guiana 1856, 1 cent black on magenta [figure 9]. The appelation is not entirely justified; although the stamp is truly unique, there are other, less

valuable stamps of which only a single specimen is known.

The stamp, one of a series printed locally when a supply of normal stamps failed to arrive from London, is unsatisfactory to the aesthete, as it has clipped corners and is rubbed on the surface, presenting a condition which would not be tolerated by discriminating collectors in a much commoner stamp. It was discovered in 1873 by twelve-year old L. Vernon Vaughan, a British Guiana schoolboy, among some old family correspondence in an attic at his home. He put the stamp in his collection, but not long afterwards, to enable him to buy some more colourful issues, sold it locally to a collector.

Then, in 1878, it was sent to Glasgow and soon afterwards was bought by that fabulous collector, Philipp la Rénotière von Ferrary, for about £50. It remained in his collection until 1922 when, at one of the fourteen Ferrary auction sales in Paris, the stamp was bought by Arthur

5 Envelope bearing two 1d Post Office Mauritius

6 (overleaf left) British Guiana: Cottonreels 4 cents on lemon yellow paper, on cover

7 (right) British Guiana: 1852 1c black on magenta

8 (far right) British Guiana: 1852 4c black on deep blue

96
20 Liv
11.6. 40
5.8. 20

W. J. Forte Esquire

Pl. Vreed en hoop

BRITISH GUIANA

9 The British Guiana 1856 1 cent

10 British Guiana: 1856 (Feb) 4c black on *blue*, a superb used copy, with large margins from the lower edge of the sheet

Hind, a millionaire American plush manufacturer.

After his death in 1933 the stamp was successfully claimed in court by his widow. Then, in 1940, she sold the rarity for an undisclosed amount, (which is rumoured to have been about £10,000 — $40,000), to the present owner, whose name has remained one of the best kept secrets in philately. In 1965 this remarkable stamp was on show at the Royal Festival Hall, London, during the Stanley Gibbons Catalogue Centenary Exhibition, and was insured for £200,000.

British Guiana had been responsible for an earlier issue which takes its place high in the list of rarities. It comprises the 'Cottonreels', so called because they are circular and resemble the labels on reels of cotton. They, too, were printed in a local newspaper office and are extremely crude; so much so that, as a safeguard against forgery, each one, like the 1 cent of 1856, was initialled by the postal clerk selling the stamp.

Rarest of the 'Cottonreels' is the 2 cents black on rose. A mere ten examples are known to exist, six of them in pairs used to make up the 4 cents postal rate. The best story about these 2 cents concerns one of the pairs on a letter addressed to 'Miss Rose, Blankenburg'. One day in 1896 the Canon of a church in Demerara appealed to members of his congregation to offer him any old stamps they might have, so that they might be sold to collectors and the proceeds used to help pay off the church's overdraft and mortgage. An old coloured lady found two early 4 cents stamps, worth a few pounds, which she sent to the clergyman. When he went to thank her for her gift, he asked whether she had any more old stamps. She answered that she had given all her stamps away, but then brought out an old basket filled with bills and receipts. As he searched through them, he came across this fine old envelope [figure 11].

The lady to whom it was addressed was in the room at the time, and, on being told that the stamps were worth a lot of money, she danced for joy and exclaimed: 'Thank

God! I am at last able to give something worthwhile.'

The envelope was sold for more than £200, which helped to clear off most of the church's debt. In 1934 the envelope was bought by the late Theodore Champion for £1,300 and since then it has not been on the market, but a rather similar cover, formerly in the Maurice Burrus collection, was auctioned by Robson Lowe Ltd in 1963 and realized £25,500.

An extremely rare 'Cottonreel' is the 4 cents on lemon yellow paper; fourteen examples have been recorded and a fine specimen on cover is in the Tapling Collection [figure 6].

In Western Australia a curious error occurred on the first 4d stamps issued in 1854. The design shows a swan in the centre, the emblem of the state being the black swan, a reminder of the days of the Swan River Settlement. The stamp, which was lithographed in one colour, blue, is known with the frame inverted in relation to the centre [figure 22], and

overleaf

12 *(above left)* Hawaii: 1851 H. I. & U. S. Postage used on cover

13 *(below left)* Hawaii: 1851 Missionary 5c

14 *(below centre)* Hawaii: 1851 13 cents

15 *(below right)* Hawaii: 1851 Missionary 'H. I. & U. S. Postage' 13c

16-21 *(right)* A choice selection of abnormals from the Royal Collection

11 The 'Miss Rose, Blankenburg' cover bearing a pair of 2 cents cottonreels

Kobe —

75921

PAID

Mr. C H Burrage
Care Welkinson Stetson Co
Milk St Boston
Ms
USA

22 Western Australia: 1854 4d Inverted Swan

only fourteen examples have been discovered. When this variety was first found by early collectors, they dubbed it the 'Inverted Swan', and that sobriquet is still colourfully used, although it has been known for many years that the frame, not the centre, was inverted.

One of the first examples of this error to become known to collectors was found in Ireland in 1863, and several years later it came into the hands of a stamp collector in Dublin. While in conversation with the Duke of Leinster in a Dublin stamp shop one day in the eighteen-seventies, a young collector by the name of Vance mentioned that he knew that the owner of the stamp was willing to sell it for £3, and the Duke, a keen philatelist, at once asked Vance to obtain it, giving him a cheque for that amount.

Young Vance had great difficulty in getting the cheque cashed; but immediately on obtaining the money, he hurried to the owner, Mr Morris, a master at Dublin High School, who was disposing of his collection piecemeal. In order to put Morris into a good humour, Vance made a few small purchases and then, on coming to the page of Western Australia, he asked whether the 'Inverted Swan' was for sale.

'Yes,' replied the master, 'you can have it for £3.' At this Vance objected to the figure quoted, argued that the stamp was probably not genuine, and was unsatisfactory in other respects. At length he succeeded in persuading Morris to part with it for £2. When Vance later handed the stamp to the Duke, he was so delighted that he gave the boy several pounds' worth of stamps as a present. After the Duke's death in 1897, Ireland received his collection as a gift, and this rarity is now on permanent exhibition at the Ard-Mhusaeum Na h-Éireann in Dublin. Another example of the error cut to the shape of its octagonal frame is in the Tapling Collection in the British Museum.

The 'inverted aeroplane' on the United States 24 cents airmail stamp of 1918 has a red frame and a blue centre showing an aircraft in flight. Two separate printing operations were necessary, and, by mistake, at least one sheet was turned upside down between the two printings, thus causing the error [figure 27]. The only sheet known to philatelists was bought at a Washington post office on Tuesday, 14 May 1918. the first day of issue. The fortunate purchaser was W.T. Robey, a stockbroker's clerk. He had arranged to exchange first-day covers with several friends in New York and Philadelphia, and withdrew $30 from the bank, went to a nearby post office and asked for a sheet of the 24 cents stamps. The clerk told Robey that only a few stamps were in stock, but another supply was expected at about mid-day. Promptly at noon he returned, passed his $24 over the counter, and the clerk handed him the sheet of 100 stamps. Robey took one look at it, and then, to quote his own words, his 'heart stood still'. All the aeroplanes were upside down!

Briefly he drew the clerk's attention to this and rushed out of the post office. The clerk hurried to the telephone. Robey returned home, hardly able to believe his good fortune. He tried to calculate how much the sheet of stamps might be worth, but could not even guess. While he was still thinking, sitting in a chair, there was a ring at the door and two postal inspectors entered his room. They questioned him about his purchase, which he would not show to them, and at first by cajoling, and then by threatening dire consequences, they tried to part him from his treasure. Robey was adamant. He completely refused to part with it, and eventually the inspectors left.

Later that day Robey showed the sheet to a nearby stamp dealer who offered $500 for it, but Robey refused. Subsequently, another dealer offered him $10,000, but this also was rejected. A few days later Robey went to New York with the intention of offering the sheet to the millionaire stamp collector Colonel E.H.R. Green, but the Colonel was away, and after several other attempts Robey negotiated with Eugene Klein, of Philadelphia, who bought the sheet on behalf of a syndicate for $15,000. Afterwards Colonel

23 *(overleaf left)* Great Britain: 1910 the 2d Tyrian plum; the page in the Royal Collection

24 *(above right)* Rare telegraph stamps of Great Britain in the Royal Collection

25 *(below right)* Great Britain: the £5 orange

Stamp printed for use.
Wmk. Imperial
Crown. Perf. 14.

Specimen passed through
the Post on May 5th, 1910,
the day before King Edward died.

To His Royal Highness
The Prince of Wales, K.G.
&c &c &c
Marlborough House
S. W.

26 The unique Sweden 1855-57 3 sk-bco error of colour

Green bought it for $20,000, but Robey was well satisfied with his bargain; he had made some $15,000 in less than a week.

The unique sheet was soon broken up into singles and blocks, some of which remain in the same condition today. Their value has risen tremendously, and by 1966 had reached about $20,000 for a single stamp, as much as Col. Green paid for the entire sheet forty-eight years previously.

An error of a different kind occurred to produce what has become known as Europe's rarest stamp, the unique Swedish 1855 3 skilling-banco, printed by mistake not in green, but in yellow, the normal colour of the 8 skilling-banco of the same set [figure 26].

The unique stamp was discovered in 1885 by a Stockholm schoolboy, Georg Wilhelm Baeckman, on an old letter of his grandfather, a keen naturalist, who one day in July 1857 received it from his brother, together with a new specimen of moss which he, also a keen naturalist, had found near the village of Nya Kopparberg. Postage on the letter, which related the story of the mossy find, had been paid by a yellow stamp, and it was this stamp which young Baeckman removed from the old envelope.

He had read an advertisement by a stamp dealer in Stockolm, offering 7 kronor for 3 skilling-banco stamps of the 1855 issue, and when the boy took his find to the dealer's shop the stamp was at first regarded with suspicion. The dealer could not understand why it was printed in yellow instead of green; he put it in water, but the stamp did not change colour, and eventually he decided to pay the boy the promised amount. Baeckman went home joyfully.

Some time afterwards the dealer publicized the 3 skilling-banco and exhibited it in Stockolm. Nine years later he sold it to a Viennese dealer, and from him it passed to Philipp la Rénotière von Ferrary for 4,000 gulden. At the Ferrary sales the error realized about £700, to change hands again for about £1,500 in 1926 and, in 1937, it was bought by

27 USA: 1918 24 cents airmail with inverted
aeroplane, a block of four

the late King Carol of Rumania for about £5,000. In 1950, the stamp was bought, together with several other rarities, by René Berlingin for a price believed to have been about £27,000.

The first stamps of Hawaii, issued in 1851, are known to philatelists as the 'Missionaries', because many of them were used on mail from missionaries in the Hawaiian Islands to relatives and friends in the United States. The stamps are of denominations of 2, 5, or 13 cents, and were crudely printed from type and ornaments set up by hand [figures 12-15, 30]. The paper used was thin and very brittle. Consequently most of the surviving specimens are damaged. Rarest is the 2 cents, of which only fifteen are known. Two are in the Tapling Collection at the British Museum; three more are in museums in Honolulu, and most of the others are in private collections. The earliest stamps bear the legend 'Hawaiian Postage' but a later variety of the 13 cents is inscribed 'H.I. & U.S. Postage'.

There is a gruesome story connected with one of the 2 cents, and although the veracity of this tale has been questioned, contemporary reports point to its being true. The story concerns the specimen formerly in the Ferrary and Burrus collections and which, in 1963, realized $41,000 at H.R. Harmer's Burrus auction in New York. In the early eighteen-nineties the stamp was in the collection of Gaston Leroux, a well known Parisian philatelist. One day he was found murdered in his flat. The crime puzzled the police, who could find no apparent motive. There was a considerable sum of money in the rooms, but none had been taken nor had a diamond-studded watch and some gold coins in a half-open drawer in a desk. The police were unable to trace that the murdered man had any enemies.

Detectives put in charge of the case were baffled, but one, who had some knowledge of stamp collecting, found a possible clue. He discovered that Leroux's collection of Hawaiian stamps, of which there was a catalogue, had one

30 Hawaii: 1851 2 cents 'Missionary'

28 (opposite above) The cover bearing the 1d and 2d Post Office Mauritius

29 (below) Mauritius: 1859 2d post paid used block of four

stamp missing: the 2 cents of 1851. The detective visited every dealer in Paris who might have been able to sell a stamp of this kind, but without result.

Eventually the detective's suspicions became centered on Hector Giroux, one of Leroux's friends, who was also a keen philatelist. The detective secured an introduction to Giroux while posing as a stamp collector, and after a time they became close companions. Unsuspectingly Giroux invited the officer to his flat, and one evening the conversation turned to the subject of rarity, especially that of the Hawaiian 'Missionaries', with the 2 cents as the star item. Enthusiastically, Giroux brought out an example of this issue, the very one for which the detective had been searching.

The following day Giroux was arrested and questioned, and when he failed to produce satisfactory evidence of the manner in which he had acquired the stamp, he was charged with the murder and brought to trial. Eventually he broke down and confessed that he had murdered his friend after he had refused to part with the 2 cents stamp needed to complete the set of 'Missionaries' in Giroux's collection.

31 Thomas Keay Tapling whose collection, now in the British Museum, contains many of the rarities described and illustrated in this book

32 Hawaii: 1851 2c and 5c together with a
pair of USA 3c used on cover

CHAPTER TWO

British rarities

THE PENNY BLACK OF 1840 is not a rare stamp, although the demand for specimens has pushed up the price far beyond that asked for substantially scarcer stamps of other issues. At the beginning of the twentieth century a fine used example of the Penny Black could be bought for no more than 3d; by 1966 the price had risen to about £3; and who can say that it will not have reached double figures by the end of the century?

This does not mean that no Penny Black is rare. The stamp was printed from eleven different plates, and whereas most of them are of more or less equal scarcity, the same does not apply to examples from plate 11. That plate was brought into use at the time when the Penny Black was being superseded by the Penny Red, and 700 sheets, a relatively small number, were printed in black. Consequently, stamps from this plate are far more valuable than specimens from the previous ten. In unused condition the plate 11 stamp is rare. Many years ago a part sheet was found and was later cut up. Probably the finest remaining piece from that sheet is a corner block of nine showing the plate number [figure 33]. Until 1956 it was in the famous collection of Great Britain formed by H. C. V. Adams.

At the time when the Penny Black was issued it was intended also to issue a special version of the stamp for use on mail from Government departments. The only difference in the design was that the upper corners were to contain,

33 (*opposite*) Great Britain: the corner block of nine Penny Blacks from Plate 11 showing the plate number

34 Great Britain: the Penny Black 'V.R.'

instead of small crosses, the letters VR [figure 34]. This stamp was never put into use, although a few examples bearing experimental cancellations are known.

More than 170 plates were employed in the production of the imperforate Penny Red. Most of these Penny Red stamps are relatively common, but there is one outstanding rarity among them. It occurs on plate 77.

These stamps, like the Penny Blacks, had letters in the lower corners, indicating the exact position of each stamp in the sheet of 240. The first stamp was lettered A-A, the second stamp A-B, the third stamp A-C, the first stamp in the second row was B-A, the second stamp B-B, and so on to T-L, which was the twelfth stamp in the twentieth row. The corner letters were hammered into the plate by the use of a hand-held punch. On plate 77 the siderographist punched the letter B on the first stamp in the second row, but omitted to add the A in the lower right corner, thus causing what philatelists refer to as the 'B-blank' variety [figure 35]. The printers did not discover and correct the mistake for about nine months. By that time thousands of sheets containing the error had been issued.

During the nineteenth century Penny Reds were extremely common, and few collectors bothered to study them. As a result it was more than fifty years before the first example of the 'B-blank' was discovered. It was first shown at an exhibition of British stamps held in London in 1905, and another example was found the following year. Since those days several dozens more have come to light, but this is a popular stamp of a popular country, and whenever specimens come on the market they realize about £400 each.

Two other errors of lettering occur on British stamps. One is the 'OP-PC' error on the 1½d of 1870. The lettering in this case appeared in the upper and lower corners, and the stamp should have been inscribed CP-PC. The error occurred because the siderographist punched the C inverted and, instead of bothering to go through the lengthy process of erasing his mistake, then drilling the back of the metal plate and hammering the surface flush to begin again, thus risking damaging the design in the process, he just turned the C round and punched it in the right way up; the slight irregularity of the two letters C can be observed on the imprimatur sheet in the British Post Office archives. Originally it had been intended to issue this value in 1860 and some sheets were printed in rosy-mauve. Afterwards it was decided not to issue the 1^{1}/$_{2}$d stamp, and it was only in 1870 that this decision was altered. A further supply was printed in rose-red, and all but one of the known examples of the error are in that colour. In used condition they are fairly scarce, and unused they are rare. The only recorded example of the error in rosy-mauve is in the Royal Collection, and is the right hand stamp in a strip of three.

The other error of lettering occurs on the 2^{1}/$_{2}$d rosy-mauve of 1873; the last stamp in the eighth row of sheets from plate no. 2 is lettered LH at the top and FL at the foot. This error is about as scarce as the OP-PC error on the 1^{1}/$_{2}$d.

Extremely rare is the Penny Red of the 1864 issue which was printed from plate no. 77. This is not to be confused with the 'B-blank' error on plate 77 of the imperforate Penny Red, as the 1864 issue is perforated and has letters in all four corners. On those stamps the plate number, in small uncoloured figures, appears in the network on each side of the Queen's head.

The numbering of plates in this series began at 69, but that plate was found to be unfit for use and no stamps were printed from it; plate 70 was also found to be faulty and was not used. The first plate used for printing issued stamps was 71. There was more trouble with plates 75 and 77, and although a few sheets were printed from plate 75, no examples have ever been found. A few sheets were printed from plate 77, and altogether nine stamps have been discovered. There is an unused specimen, lettered BA-AB, in the Royal Collection, and another lettered AB-BA in the Tapling collection.

35 Great Britain: the Penny Red B-blank

A third unused example lettered CA-AC was found in 1919, and years later it passed into the collection of J. de R. Phillp. At the sale of his collection in 1959 this stamp realized £1,700, and was subsequently acquired by Major C.E. Raphael. In February 1965 the Major's collection of Great Britain was stolen and the present whereabouts of this plate 77 are unknown. Unless it has been destroyed, it must come to light sooner or later, and if ever it is put on the market its identity will be recognized immediately, because it is the only example of plate no. 77 lettered CA-AC.

The existence of one other unused specimen of plate no. 77 has been recorded, but the lettering is not known to the authors. Of the five recorded used specimens, one, lettered IP-PI, is on a small piece of envelope together with a 4d stamp; this, too, was once in the J. de R. Phillp collection. One of the used examples was contained in a collection destroyed in the San Francisco earthquake of 1906.

A group of mid-Victorian stamps which contains many rarities is that known as the 'Abnormals'. These were stamps printed from plates not issued in the normal course of events. A few registration sheets were printed, and in some cases were perforated and put into stock, and it is from these sheets that the 'Abnormals' came [figures 16-21]. They comprise the following stamps: *1862 issue* – 3d with white dots just below the floral ornaments on each side of the Queen's head; 9d with hair-lines across the outer angles of the corner squares; 1s plate no. 2; *1865-7 issue* – 9d plate no. 5; *1867-80 issue* – 6d plate no. 10; 10d plate no. 2; 2s plate no. 3; *1872-3 issue* – 6d pale chestnut plate no. 12; *1873-80 issue* – 6d pale buff plate no. 13; 1s green plate no. 14; 4d vermilion plate no. 16; 4d sage green plate no. 17.

Rarest of all is the 1s green plate no. 14, of which only four examples have been found. One is in the Royal Collection and another, perhaps the finest, was formerly in the collection of H. C. V. Adams. That collection contained also four examples have been found. One is in the Royal Collection and another, perhaps the finest, was formerly in the collection of H. C. V. Adams, which contained also one of the six or seven recorded specimens of the 6d plate 10, a glorious example used on an envelope from Weymouth to Florence.

In 1935 a used example of this 6d plate 10 was discovered in Hollywood, California, and was sent to London, where it was auctioned by H. R. Harmer Ltd. At that time the sum realized by the stamp £155, was considered quite substantial and reports of the sale appeared in newspapers in many parts of the world. One of these reports was read by a philatelist in Austria, who at once went to his own collection to see whether, by some chance, he had one of the rarities. Sure enough, he did! Soon afterwards that specimen, too, was offered by the same auctioneers and realised £190.

Another stamp which is sometimes considered to be an 'Abnormal', but is in fact an error of paper, is the 1865-67 10d red-brown, plate 1, printed on paper watermarked with heraldic emblems instead of a spray of rose [figure 36]. This error was due entirely to the printers, who disobeyed instructions and used the wrong paper. Only nine examples, six bearing Constantinople postmarks, have been recorded.

Before 1867 the highest value postage stamp issued by the British Post Office had a face value of 2s, but in that year 5s stamps were put on·sale, to be followed within the next 15 years by 10s, £1 and £5 values. That £5 [figure 25], printed in orange, at first on blued paper and later on white paper, has remained to this day the highest value postage stamp ever issued in Great Britain. Unused examples of all these high values are rare.

Three notable rarities, one of them in the unobtainable class, occur on stamps of King Edward VII. In those days experimental printings were being made, and two colour varieties emerged which are now extremely scarce: the 3d in grey on lemon coloured paper instead of purple on lemon, and the 6d in bright magenta on chalk surfaced paper. The second of these is known only unused.

36 Great Britain: 1865-67 10d on 'Emblems' paper, used at Constantinople (C in bars)

37 Great Britain: 1873-80 4d vermilion, plate 16

Shortly before King Edward died it was decided to issue all the low value stamps of Great Britain in single colours. The 7d had already appeared on 4 May 1910, and it had been planned to issue the 2d on 6 May in a new design, printed in what is known as Tyrian plum. Supplies had been distributed to post offices, but, when the King died on 6 May, were withdrawn; before that happened, however, a friend of the Prince of Wales obtained a specimen of the 2d Tyrian plum, stuck it on a letter and posted it to His Royal Highness. The letter was duly delivered, bearing the only known used example of this rare stamp. The letter is now in the Royal Collection, which also contains an unused pair [figure 23]. A few other unused examples are in private hands and there is an almost complete sheet in the General Post Office.

The early stamps of King George v include the $^1/_2$d and the 1d in the three-quarter face type, perforated 14 instead of 15 x 14. It has been stated that the variety occurred when, under great pressure of work, the printers obtained permission by telephone to use one of the perforating machines employed for Edwardian stamps. The $^1/_2$d with this perforation was issued at several places, mostly on the coast of East Anglia, and, in unused condition, this value is extremely rare, although used copies, fairly expensive, are not too difficult to find. Only four or five unused specimens of the 1d are known, and there is no record of any used copies.

The 1935 Silver Jubilee issue contains a rarity, the 2$^1/_2$d in Prussian blue instead of the normal ultramarine. Some three sheets were found in a North London post office and bought by a philatelist who offered some of the stamps to a leading firm of stamp dealers. After considering the matter for some time they returned the stamps to him. Later they were offered to another firm which bought his entire holding of 319 specimens, and shortly afterwards they were advertised in the philatelic press at £5 each. At that price they sold rapidly and the figure was soon increased. In 1966 this stamp realized about £80 at auction. The colour was not an

38 Great Britain: 1941 2$^1/_2$d faultily cut booklet page showing tête-bêche

error in itself; the stamps are believed to have been colour trials which were issued by mistake to a post office.

The stamps of King George VI include several errors of perforation. In the 1937 issue the 1½d, 4d, 5d, 7d, and 10d are known imperforate all round or on three sides, and the 1941 ½d, 1d [figure 39], 2d and 2½d exist in similar condition, as do the 1950 ½d, 1d and 2d. Some values of these issues have been found also in tête-bêche pairs, and these came mostly from booklets faultily cut during manufacture [figure 38]. Stamps are printed in sheets normally containing the tête-bêche arrangement specially for binding in the booklets, as this arrangement facilitates the stitching and cutting, but in normal circumstances such pairs and blocks do not reach the public.

39 Great Britain: 1941 1d, a part sheet part imperforate

40 Great Britain: 1961 2¹/₂d with Missing Head and undenominated error

Quite a large number of errors and varieties, many of them rare, occur on the stamps of Queen Elizabeth II. Apart from the imperforate and tête-bêche varieties, which have been found on several of the low value definitives issued between 1952 and 1966, there is a range of 'missing colour' 'errors' on the commemorative stamps.

These 'errors' are in a special class in that their occurrence is an everyday inevitable happening in the course of printing; the vast majority of them are observed and extracted by the checkers, who scan each sheet at the end of the production line; because of their extreme efficiency, 'errors' on the market are rare, as the prices they command testify.

Before 1960 all British commemoratives had been printed in single colours, but in that year the two Europa stamps were the first to be issued in two colours. They were followed during the next few years by stamps in three and four colours, and multi-colour photogravure has now become a firm favourite with the British stamp printers.

The first outstanding example of colours, and consequently parts of designs, being omitted occured on the 6d of the Seventh Commonwealth Parliamentary Conference issue of 1961. Normally this stamp was printed in purple and gold, but specimens were found in which the gold printing was missing, and they came on the market at substantial prices.

Much more spectacular was the 'error' which occured on the 3d of the 1962 National Productivity Year set. This variety, known as the 'Headless Queen', shows the Queen's portrait completely omitted from the oval space at the right of the stamp [figure 41]. A block of seventy-six examples of this 'error' was acquired by Stanley Gibbons Ltd and offered for sale at the Stamp Exhibition in March 1963, priced at £85 each. Within two days all had been sold. Before the end of the exhibition week specimens were changing hands at £150 and since then the price has about doubled. A similar 'error' occurred on the 1s 3d of the same issue; it was discovered by a US serviceman attached to the Northolt,

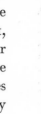

Middlesex, Air Base. He bought a vertical block of twelve of the 1s 3d stamps at a post office in Harrow and found that, although the upper ten stamps were normal, the corner pair had the head missing. Another similar pair was bought the next day from the same post office and a few other examples have been found as well. The original pair was auctioned by H. R. Harmer Ltd in 1963 and realized £775.

Not long afterwards another 'Missing Head' variety was found, on the 2½d of the 1961 Post Office Savings Bank Centenary issue [figure 40]. The stamp had been part of a purchase made by a business man at Rochester, Kent. He was not particularly interested in stamps, but when these were handed to him he noticed that the Queen's head was missing. He tore one off and put it in his wallet, giving the others to his secretary to put in a safe place; she put them in a correspondence file. He thought nothing more of it until 1963, when the publicity given to the 'Headless Queen' reminded him of it. He searched for the stamps, but discovered to his dismay that the file had been cleared, and the papers it had contained had been thrown away. However, he still had the single specimen in his wallet, and although the stamp was by then rubbed and soiled, he sold it for a substantial amount to Bridger and Kay Ltd, the London dealers. This is the only example of the 'error' known to philatelists. The denomination is also omitted.

Another remarkable error, and the second one of its kind to have occurred so far on a British stamp, is the 'undenominated' variety on the 4d of the International Geographical Congress

41 Great Britain: 1962 National Productivity Year 3d showing the Headless Queen error

42 Great Britain: 1964 Forth Bridge 6d blue colour omitted (*stamp at foot*)

43 (*opposite*) Great Britain: 1964 International Geographical Congress 4d half sheet showing value omitted, the second error of this kind ever to occur on a stamp of Great Britain

issue of 1964. Normally this stamp was printed in five colours: orange-brown, red-brown, rose, black and violet. The denomination and a small part of the central design were in violet. Half a sheet, bought in a Leicester post office, was found to have the violet colour, and consequently the value, completely missing. Subsequently two other half-sheets showing the same error were found [figure 43]. The stamp was offered at first at £85, but the price has risen since then.

The 1963 Red Cross Centenary issue has a red cross as a prominent feature of the design, and the 3d has been found with the cross entirely omitted. Another missing colour occurs on the 6d of the Forth Road Bridge issue of 1964. This was discovered by a Scottish schoolboy, Colin Sherriff, when he bought one of the stamps at a Dunfermline post office on the day of issue. He noticed immediately that the blue colour, which should have run vertically up the stamp, was missing, and he recognized the variety as an 'error'. As a keen philatelist he stuck the stamp on a letter addressed to himself and posted it. The next day it arrived complete with first day postmark [figure 42].

He did not keep the news of his discovery to himself and another collector was able to buy several more examples of the same 'error' from the post office, but it was Colin's discovery which made the headlines and was featured on radio and television. Not long afterwards he decided to part with his treasure and went to London to attend the auction; after keen bidding, his precious envelope realized £380.

Mention has already been made of the Penny Black with V R in the upper corners, which it was intended to issue as a stamp for use by Government departments but which remained unissued. Not until 1882 were special stamps produced for such official use. Then some denominations of ordinary postage stamps were overprinted with the legend 'I. R. Official' for use by the Inland Revenue. They were followed during the next few years by stamps with other overprints, such as 'Govt. Parcels' and 'O. W. Official' for

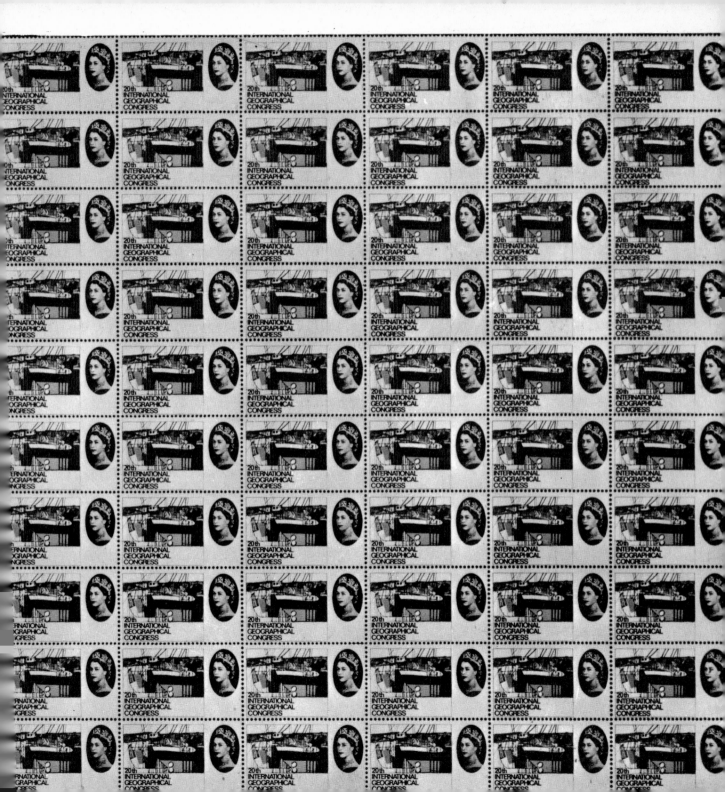

44 Great Britain: 1904 6d I.R. Official
45 Great Britain: 1902-04 10s I.R. Official
46 (*opposite above left*) Barbados: 1863 1s blue error of colour
47 (*above right*) Gold Coast: 1889 20s red and green
48 (*below*) Cape of Good Hope: pair of Woodblocks with one stamp the 4d red error of colour

use, respectively, on Government parcels and by the Office of Works. The War Office, too, had its own specially over-printed stamps ('Army Official'), and in the reign of King Edward VII stamps were overprinted also for the Admiralty, the Royal Household and the Board of Education.

Some of these official stamps are extremely rare. Rarest of all is the Edward VII 6d purple, overprinted I. R. Official [figure 44], of which only about a dozen specimens are known. The stamp is rare because it was issued on the very day (14 May 1904) that an order came into effect with-drawing all official stamps from use. There are an unused pair and single and a used single of this 6d stamp in the Royal Collection, an unused block of four in the Árd-Mhu-saeum Nah-Éireann in Dublin, and a few other examples in private hands. There is an almost complete sheet (234 stamps) in the General Post Office. A single unused example was auctioned by Harmer, Rooke & Co., Ltd in 1964 for £3,200.

Another rarity in the same series is the 10s of Edward VII [figure 45], of which about thirty copies are known, most of them unused; in addition there is a large part sheet in the General Post Office. The £1 values of Queen Victoria and King Edward VII with the same overprint are also rarities, as is the Edward 1s overprinted 'Board of Education'.

Two very rare errors among the Officials are the Queen Victoria Government Parcels 1891-1900 1s green and car-mine with the overprint 'Govt. Parcels' inverted, and the Ed-ward VII 1d overprinted 'Official', with the word 'Army' omitted. The Victorian 1s has a curious history; although the error was discovered about the beginning of the twentieth century, a few years later all the existing specimens were condemned as forgeries, and the variety was deleted from the catalogues. In the nineteen-forties a few examples, still affixed to wrapping paper and well tied by the postmarks, came into the possession of Harry Nissen, the London dealer, and after being carefully examined, were pronounced to be genuine; the error then had its catalogue status restored.

CHAPTER THREE

British Commonwealth rarities

TWO OF THE RAREST STAMPS of the British Commonwealth were never put on sale at post offices. The Barbados
1s blue in the 'Britannia' type was an error pure and simple.
Normally this stamp was printed in black. A supply of
50,000 copies sent to the Island in 1863 was found on ar-
rival to be printed in blue [figure 46]. The printers were
notified of the error and they sent another supply in the
correct colour. The blue stamps were not put on sale, and it
is uncertain what happened to them, but a few reached the
hands of collectors and there is one in the Tapling Collection. It is believed that fewer than a dozen have survived.

The other unissued stamp is the so-called 'Connell' of
New Brunswick which was prepared in 1860, when that
Canadian province went over to decimal currency, so that a
new series of stamps was needed. Charles Connell, the Postmaster-General, made arrangements with the printers to
put the portrait of Queen Victoria on the 10 cents, while the
head of the Prince of Wales was to appear on the 17 cents,
the 1 cent was to show a locomotive, and the 12$\frac{1}{2}$ cents a
steamship. For the most commonly used 5 cents Connell
selected his own portrait!

When the stamps were delivered they were shown to the
Governor of New Brunswick, who was shocked. After ur-
gent messages were exchanged between the Governor and
Charles Connell, the issue of stamps was delayed until the

49a Bermuda: Thies's issue

49 (opposite) Bermuda: 1865 1d imperforate

50 (overleaf above left) Mauritius: 1859 2d
post paid

51 (above centre) Samoa: 1914 (3 September)
1 Shilling on 1 m

52 (above right) Togo: British Issues 1915
(7 January) 50 pf

53 (below left) India: 1854 4as unique cover
bearing two inverted heads

54 (overleaf right) Ceylon: 1859 4d dull rose

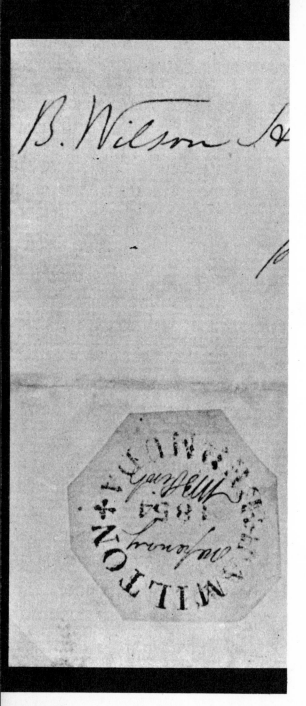

Council could meet. The meeting took place a few days afterwards and subsequently Connell placed his resignation in the hands of the Governor. A new 5 cents stamp bearing the Queen's portrait was ordered, and Connell bought up the 5,000 sheets, each of 100 stamps, showing his own picture. One evening he made a huge bonfire of them in the garden of his country house, and the few examples which he had presented to collectors or kept as mementoes before the holocaust are all that remain to remind philatelists of one of the most curious events in philatelic history.

A postmaster who issued his own stamps without any objection being raised was William B. Perot, of Hamilton Bermuda. He was part-time Postmaster from 1818 until 1862, and from 1846 onwards he was granted an annual salary of £70 in addition to any inland postage he might collect.

Perot was a keen gardener and lived in a house, now a museum, at the entrance to Par-la-Ville Park. People would come at all times of the day to hand in their letters, together with pennies to pay postage, and often Perot would have to leave his garden in order to attend to the post office. For the convenience of those who wanted to post letters at night, he installed a box into which letters and money could be dropped. When he opened the box in the morning, however, he found sometimes that there were more letters than pennies to pay for them, and, of course, nothing to identify the absent-minded, ignorant or deceitful.

By 1848 this had assumed such proportions that he discussed the matter with a friend, who suggested that a stamp or label might be prepared and sold at a penny so that people posting letters in the box could frank them with a stamp and so show that Perot had been prepaid his penny postage. Perot made his stamps by striking his postmarking handstamp several times on sheets of paper, which were supplied with gum, and wrote the words 'one penny' in the centre above the year adding his signature below [figure 56]. At first he used black ink on his handstamp, but about 1849 he changed

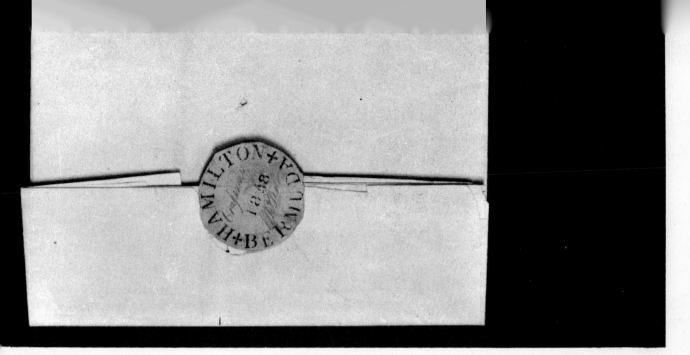

to red. The stamps were a great success and his emoluments increased accordingly.

Only eleven of these rare and curious stamps have ever been found. Two, dated 1853, on thick white paper, and cut almost circular, formed the only recorded unsevered pair, but it was separated in 1934. Two are on entire letters and they are both in a well-known collection in Hamilton; and the same collection also contains three other specimens. There are three more in the Royal Collection.

Shortly before his term of office ended Perot used a different handstamp, consisting of a crowned circle with 'Paid at Hamilton, Bermuda' in the centre. This had been used as a postmark on mail, but is known struck on pieces of paper used as adhesive stamps. Only four of this second type have been found. Adhesives of a similar kind, but inscribed 'Paid at St. Georges, Bermuda' were used by J. H. Thies, Postmaster of that town, in the early eighteen-sixties. No more than four examples of these are known [figure 49a].

The prepayment of postage by means of stamps was authorized in Canada early in April 1851, but at that time

56 Bermuda: Perot's first issue used on the back of a letter

55 (opposite) Bermuda: 1848-54 'Perot Issue' 1d in red. A letter-sheet addressed to 'B. Wilson Higgs Esq., St Georges', with the Perot stamp affixed to the back of the fold

57 (overleaf left) Austria: the Red Mercury

58 Saxony: 1850 3 pfennig red

59 Switzerland: the Basle Dove in marginal pair

60 (overleaf above right) Saxony: 1851 a used pair of the 1/2 neugroschen error of colour

61 (overleaf below right) Switzerland: the Double Geneva

62 Canada: unused pair of the 12d black

63 Canada: 1959 Seaway 5 cents with inverted centre

no stamps had been provided. For a short while before supplies became available, R. W. Kelly, Postmaster of New Carlisle, Gaspé, had some envelopes printed in black with the words 'Three Pence' enclosed in an ornamental frame, and used them to denote the prepayment of postage. Only one such envelope has been found [figure 64].

Canada's most famous rarity is the 12d black of 1851 [figure 62]. It is inscribed 'Twelve Pence' instead of 'One Shilling', because, unlike that of the penny, the value of a shilling differed in various parts of North America: in New England it was equal to 10d, while in New York its value was no more than 7$\frac{1}{2}$d. The term twelve pence admitted of no misunderstanding.

The 12d, highest denomination in Canada's first issue [figure 62] of three stamps, was little used. In the few years it was on sale only 1,510 examples were sold. In 1857 the 49,490 stamps comprising the remainders were withdrawn and destroyed. Consequently the black stamp was in short supply on the philatelic market right from the beginning and in 1865 collectors paid as much as £1 each for specimens, an extraordinary price for any stamp in those days. Despite its rarity it has been estimated that at least 50 examples, used and unused, have survived, and there are three unused pairs.

Another Canadian rarity is of much more recent origin, the 1959 5 cents stamp to mark the opening of the St. Lawrence Seaway; it exists with the centre inverted [figure 63]. The stamp was printed in red and blue, thus necessitating two separate printing operations. On 20 August 1959 an office boy was sent to the nearest Winnipeg post office to buy thirty 5 cents stamps. The office was in a department store, where the postal clerk took the uppermost sheet of fifty of the Seaway stamps from a file, tore off thirty and handed them to the boy. Back in his office he gave them to the girl in charge of mail, who removed three and affixed them to letters which the boy at once posted. Other letters

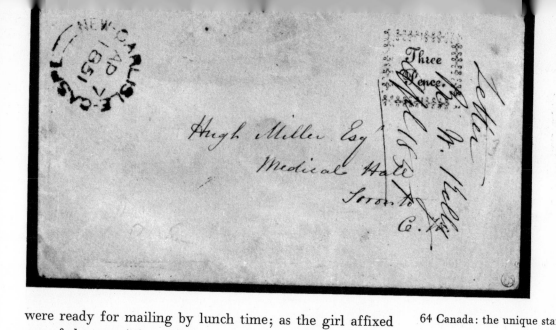

64 Canada: the unique stamp of New Carlisle

were ready for mailing by lunch time; as the girl affixed one of the remaining stamps to the first envelope, she was suddenly struck by the fact that the central design was up-side-down. A few days later another part-sheet of twenty-eight turned up at Picton, Ontario, and subsequently two more complete sheets of fifty were discovered in post office stocks; those two sheets were withdrawn from use and returned to Ottawa. Canada is a very popular country with philatelists, and the demand for specimens of the 'Seaway Invert' has caused the price to reach a considerable sum.

Ever since the earliest days of philately the triangular stamps of the Cape of Good Hope have captured the imagination of collectors. With a few notable exceptions these stamps are not specially rare, but demand for them has kept up the price.

Two of the rarest triangulars are the so-called 'Woodblock' errors: 1d blue and 4d red, instead of 1d red and 4d blue [figure 48]. The normal triangulars were printed in London, but the 'Woodblocks' were produced locally at the Cape during a stamp shortage in 1861.

The printing plates were made up of individual stereos, and by mistake a 1d stereo was put into the 4d plate, and a

65, 66 (*overleaf above left*) Naples: 1860 Trinacria and Savoy Cross

67 (*below left*) France: 1853-61 1 franc, a tête-bêche pair

68 (*right*) Spain: 1851 2 reales blue, error of colour

69 (*far right*) Sweden: 1879 20 öre Tretio error (*lowest stamp*)

51

72 Cape of Good Hope: a block of four Woodblocks with one stamp the 4d red error of colour

73 Cape of Good Hope: Woodblock 4d tête-bêche

74 Cape of Good Hope: 4d black—the mystery stamp

4d stereo into the 1d plate. The total number of 1d errors was 1,194, and there were 1,568 of the 4d in the wrong colour. In the course of time only a small percentage of these numbers has survived destruction, but two of the finest known pieces are blocks of four in red, consisting of three 1d stamps and one 4d [figure 72].

An even rarer error in the same issue is the so-called tête-bêche pair of the 4d 'Woodblock', which was discovered about 1930. This error occurred when one of the stereos worked loose and was carelessly put back into the plate so that the pair shows one stamp half inverted in relation to its neighbour. The only known example of the error, auctioned by H. R. Harmer in 1930, realized £260 [figure 73].

Extremely rare, too, is the mysterious 4d black triangular [figure 74], of which only ten copies have been recorded. One of them is in the Royal Collection and another in the Dr E. Mosely Collection in the British Museum. This variety, which is on watermarked paper like the normally issued stamps, first became known to philatelists in the early eighteen-sixties. Later it was unthinkingly stated that the stamps were issued in black for a short time as a token of mourning for Albert, the Prince Consort, but since the dates were irreconcilable this theory was seen to be nonsense. The reason why some 4d stamps were issued in black, instead of the normal blue, has never been discovered, but that specimens in the sombre hue were issued and used seems evident from the fact that some bearing postmarks are known. It is possible that the existing specimens came from proof sheets which were put into use in error.

The early stamps of Ceylon, like many other Commonwealth issues, were printed by Perkins, Bacon & Co. in London. The first stamps were imperforate and most of them are rare, but particularly rare is the 4d dull rose in unused condition [figure 54], of which probably fewer than a dozen exist; among them is an unused pair in mint condition and with full gum.

In March 1886 Dominica, in the West Indies, ran short of $^1/_2$d and 1d stamps, and in order to overcome the shortage, it was decided to surcharge the then current 6d green and 1s magenta respectively with the words 'Half Penny' and 'One Penny'. By mistake one sheet of sixty of the 6d was surcharged 'One Penny' [figure 75], and about a dozen specimens are known to exist, most of them used.

75 Dominica: 1886 One Penny on 6d error

The 1889 issue of Gibraltar includes a considerable rarity: the 10 centimos, carmine, with value omitted [figure 76]. Although these stamps are in what seems to be one colour, they were printed in more than one operation, for otherwise the error could not have occurred on a sheet. The main part of the design, showing the Queen's portrait and the framework, was printed and then the name at the top and the value at the foot were added.

The error came to light when a Gibraltar businessman sent out for some 10 centimos stamps and on receiving them was astounded to see that they bore no value. He was no philatelist, but he realized that the stamps, literally valueless, must be valuable, so he promptly sent back to the post office for more. However, by that time they had been noticed and withdrawn, and he had to be satisfied with the few copies contained in his purchase. This error is known only in unused condition, and the surviving specimens include a pair with margins from the corner of the sheet.

76 Gibraltar: 1889 10 centimos value omitted in marginal corner pair

A stamp shortage at the Gold Coast in 1883 led to the creation of the world's rarest provisional: 1d on 4d magenta. Only one example is definitely known to exist, and it is to be seen in the Tapling Collection at the British Museum; the existence of another copy has been rumoured but not confirmed. The status of this provisional has been queried, and the proof of its authenticity rests in a letter from a reader of the *Philatelic Record* of June 1883, where it is stated that confirmation had been received from a postal official of the Gold Coast itself that the provisional was in fact a genuine issue. Intensive research in the archives by one of

the authors when on local leave from military duties in 1943, although producing abundant confirmation of a stamp famine there in 1883, which was worsened by Accra stamp stocks sticking together, revealed no direct evidence of the issue of the 1d on 4d. The surcharge on the Tapling example is somewhat out of register, and it has been suggested that the figure of value was handstamped.

Another Gold Coast rarity, although not in the same class as that just mentioned, is the 20s red and green of 1889 [figure 47]. It was the Gold Coast's first stamp of this denomination, and was used mostly for fiscal purposes, although inscribed with the word 'Postage'. It became rare as a result of the theft of twenty-four sheets from a strong-room by a cleaner. The thief disposed of some of the stamps, and the theft was not discovered until two months after it occurred. Orders were issued that the 20s red and green was to be withdrawn from use, and later it was replaced by a stamp in other colours. The thief and his accomplices were tried and convicted, and about 1,000 of the missing stamps were recovered. They and the remainders were destroyed, and this accounts for the rarity of surviving specimens, which are recorded only unused.

The first postage stamps issued in India appeared in 1852, under the authority of Sir H. Bartle Frere, the Commissioner of Scinde, and were used by the Scinde District Dawk. They were small circular stamps, having as their design the seal of the East India Company, and were issued in white, in blue and in red [figures 82, 83, 84]. The white and blue stamps were embossed on paper, but the red were embossed on wafers and are the rarest of all. Owing to the brittle nature of the wafers, most of the specimens in red which still survive are more or less damaged.

The first government issue of India appeared in 1854 and consisted of $1/2$, 1, 2 and 4 annas values. The 4 annas, showing Queen Victoria's head enclosed in an octagonal frame, was lithographed in red and blue. The red frames

78 (opposite above left) Tuscany: 1860 3 lire buff

79 (above right) Turkish Admiralty Steamship Company 3 piastres

80, 81 (below) Moldavia: 1858 81 parales and 108 parales

57

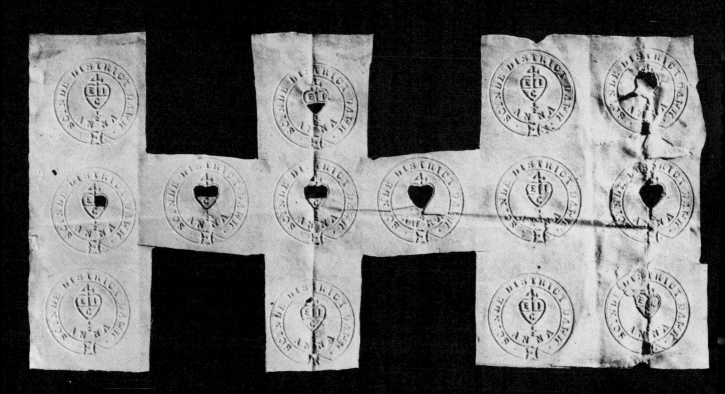

were printed first and in a few cases the sheets were fed into the press inadvertently upside-down before the blue heads were added, thus causing what collectors call the 'Indian 4 annas Inverted Head'.

The error seems not to have been known to the very early philatelists and is not mentioned in the earliest catalogues. The first time that it was referred to in the philatelic press was in 1874, when an example was shown at a meeting of the Philatelic Society, London. Twenty-five years later a remarkable find of 'Inverted Heads' was made when a resident of Southampton offered Stanley Gibbons Ltd a bundle of old correspondence, which they bought at an agreed price for every item. Some of the letters bore Indian 4 annas stamps, and on one there were two single examples of the 'Inverted Head'. Both were cut to shape, but they were well tied to the letter. As nobody seemed to want to pay the price asked for the letter, the rarities were later separated and sold singly. Another letter bearing two of these errors was bought by Thomas Keay Tapling in 1890 and can be seen at the British Museum [figure 53].

The finest existing specimen of the error [figure 85], cut square, and with margins on all sides, was discovered in a very small collection in 1954. The collection had been given to Miss Mary Lynch, of New Zealand by her great-aunt, in 1934, while she was at school. Later the young lady noticed an illustration of the 'Inverted Head' in a children's encyclopedia, but could not quite convince herself that her own specimen was genuine. When she came to England she decided to put it to the test, and showed the stamp to H.R. Harmer. She was assured that it was indeed genuine. It was auctioned on 12 October 1954 and realized £725; the present value is very substantially more.

An inverted frame error can be found on the Jamaican 1s of 1922. The stamp was printed in orange-yellow and red-orange and depicts a statue of Queen Victoria, and by mistake a sheet was printed with the frame inverted [figure

85 India: 1854 4 annas Inverted Head found in New Zealand

82 (*opposite above*) India: 1852 the white Scinde Dawk, largest known multiple

83 (*below left*) India: 1852 the blue Scinde Dawk

84 (*below right*) India: 1852 the red Scinde Dawk

86 Jamaica: 1922 1s with inverted frame

87 Lagos: 1893 Half Penny on 2d, the only known used copy

88 Niger Coast: 1893 20s on 1s

86]. A stamp collector at Manchioneal bought several 1s stamps one day in March 1922, and on examining them he found that the frames were upside-down. Returning to the post office he bought all the remaining 1s stamps in stock, but only one part sheet showed the error. The stamps were soon bought by a London dealer, and since then no others have come to light. Altogether it is believed that about twenty of them exist, among them two unused blocks of four and a few used examples. Over the years the price has risen steadily, and by 1966 had reached about £1,000.

A little-known error with an obscure history occurs in the 1893 issue of Lagos. In that year a shortage of $^1/_2$d stamps led to the surcharging of the current 4d with the words 'HALF PENNY'. At some time during the printing a sheet of 2d stamps was put through the press, and this led to the creation of the error: HALF PENNY on 2d. Until 1952 only one example, in used condition, had been recorded, but in the summer of that year a dealer discovered an unused specimen in a small collection which a London doctor had asked him to sell.

The same part of West Africa was the scene of a number of rare provisional issues, also during 1893. They were stamps of the Niger Coast, or Oil Rivers Protectorate, as it was then known. Stamps of Great Britain were overprinted for use in the territory and they formed the basic stamps on which the provisional surcharges were printed. It is the high value provisionals which are rarest, particularly the 20s on 1s [figure 88]. The surchage was applied in violet, in vermilion and in black. Only some three examples in each colour are known to exist.

During the reign of King Edward VII several British Commonwealth countries issued stamps of very high face value. They were intended almost exclusively for fiscal use, but the fact that they bear the word 'Postage' in the design has made them collectable items from the point of view of rich philatelists. One such stamp is the £25 green and carmine issued by Northern Nigeria in April 1904 [figure 89]. This is reputedly the rarest stamp of the reign. It is known only in unused condition and a specimen realized £4,500 when auctioned by Harmer, Rooke & Co., Ltd on 27 November 1964.

Another stamp in the same category is the $500 purple and orange of Straits Settlements (Malaya), issued in 1910 [figure 90], and this is certainly no more often seen than the Northern Nigerian stamp. Curiously, the £25 of Nyasaland, which had been issued during Queen Victoria's reign, is commoner.

The rarest stamps of that country (known in those days as British Central Africa) are the 2d dull and bright purple, and the green and black 4d of 1907 on paper watermarked multiple Crown CA [figure 91]. At that time the watermarked paper used for many British Commonwealth stamps was being changed from single to multiple Crown CA. In British Central Africa the 1d and 6d had already appeared on the new paper; the 2d and 4d were about to be issued when the name of the territory was changed to Nyasaland Protectorate and a new series of stamps was prepared. Whether or not the two denominations mentioned were ever actually on sale at post offices must be open to doubt, but certainly a number of these stamps came into the hands of collectors.

In 1870 a change in postal rates in South Australia meant that a 3d stamp was needed and this value was created by printing the current purple 4d in blue and surcharging it with '3-PENCE'. This surcharge was used for twenty-one years. In 1879 parts of several sheets missed the surcharging, thus giving rise to what is often known as the 4d blue error of colour, but which is more correctly described as 'surcharge omitted' [figure 133].

The error was discovered in the same year as it was issued and several examples were sold by Miss Fernley, a stamp dealer in the City of London. One of these stamps was

89 Northern Nigeria: 1904 £25

90 Straits Settlements (Malaya): 1910 500 dollars

91 Nyasaland: 1907 2d and 4d watermark multiple CA

bought by T.K. Tapling and is now in the British Museum; another was in the Ferrary Collection. A fine unused pair was bought by Stanley Gibbons Ltd about the turn of the century, but the firm separated the stamps, the right-hand specimen later going into the Royal Collection, and the left-hand example into the collection of A.H. Caspary. At the Caspary sales in 1958 this stamp realized £750. Altogether only about a dozen of the errors are known to exist. The early stamps of the Virgin Islands include a 1s black and red. Like the other early types of this colony, the main feature of the design is St Ursula. About 1890 the 1s stamp was found with the saint's figure omitted, and was promptly dubbed 'The Missing Virgin'. There is some doubt whether the variety was ever issued and it was probably a proof impression of the framework only. Examples are keenly sought and invariably realize high prices.

During the First World War provisional issues were made in a number of the German colonies captured by the Allies, and some of these stamps have proved to be extremely rare. Outstanding among them is the Cameroons 3s on 3 marks violet-black with the surcharge double and the letter 's' of '3s' inverted. A solitary specimen of this error was produced: it occurred only once in a pane of twenty of that

92 British Honduras: 1866 6d rose and 1s green se-tenant in a block of eight with inter-pane gutter

value on which the surcharge was doubly printed. The 1d on 10 pfennigs red and the 2¹/₂d on 25 pfennigs black and red on yellow of the same issue also exist with the overprint double, and only about ten of each have been recorded.

Togoland was occupied jointly by British and French forces, and each administration overprinted captured German colonial stamps with appropriate inscriptions. The first British issue includes great rarities in the 50 pfennigs and also the mark values, and the same denominations of the French issue are likewise extremely rare. It is on record that only two examples exist of the British 3 and 5 marks; there is a solitary specimen of the French 1 mark, seven of the 2 marks, two of the 3 marks, and three of the 5 marks.

93 New South Wales: 1850 2d ultramarine, plate 3, pair tête-bêche on cover

CHAPTER FOUR

European rarities

THE ISSUES OF AUSTRIA provide a number of very rare items for the connoisseur. The first stamps of that country appeared on 1 June 1850. There were five denominations, each printed in imperforate panes of sixty-four with four panes to the sheet. In those days the currency was 60 kreuzer to 1 gulden, and in order to simplify accountancy, the panes contained sixty stamps, and four spaces in the last row were filled with St Andrew's crosses.

The crosses had no postal significance, and as a rule were cut off and discarded, but in some cases the stamps and the crosses would be affixed to a letter just as they were. Even during the nineteenth century collectors found it difficult to obtain stamps with the crosses attached, but there was a big demand for such specimens, a demand which with the passage of years became more and more impossible to meet. Even the crosses themselves without stamps attached were collected and still are. The Ferrary Collection contained quite a number of stamps with crosses attached, particularly fine pieces being blocks of seven each of the 6 kreuzer and 9 kreuzer with two crosses.

In the same design as the first Austrian stamps, but with values in centesimi instead of kreuzer, was the first issue of Austrian Italy (Lombardo Venetia). Those stamps, too, can be found with St Andrew's crosses, and they are extremely rare, but rarest of all is an outstanding item, at

96 Finland: 1866 5 pen deep brown on pale lilac, tête-bêche pair

94 *(opposite above)* Switzerland: 1882-98 5c marone, tête-bêche pair

95 *(below)* Libia: parcel post stamps, 1927-39 5c brown

65

97 Austrian Italy: 1850 5 centesimi pair
showing inverted cliché

present in the Rivolta collection, consisting of two examples
of the 5 centesimi, printed on both sides of the paper. The
5 centesimi and the Austrian 1 kreuzer of this issue can be
found printed on both sides, and are not normally very rare.
The stamps were printed in orange-yellow and the colour
used during one printing was found to be too pale, so the
printed sheets were reversed and new impressions made in a
deeper shade. The two examples of the 5 centesimi already
mentioned show parts of the paler stamps on the back and,
wonderful to relate, one of the impressions is inverted in
relation to its neighbours [figure 97]. When the printing
plate of the 5 centesimi was constructed, one cliché must
have been inserted upside-down, and thus gave rise to this
remarkable variety. Curiously, no complete example showing the inverted cliché has ever been found, and its existence is proved only by these two Rivolta examples. The normally printed stamps constitute a reconstructed pair which
had been cut apart before use. The left-hand stamp was
acquired by Dr A. Rivolta's father about 1910, and the
matching right-hand specimen was discovered by Dr Rivolta himself in the nineteen-thirties, curiously enough on
an anniversary of his father's death.

In 1863 Austria issued a set of stamps in an oval embossed design, showing the Austrian arms. The values range
from 2 to 15 kreuzer, and at first these stamps were perforated 14. Later in the year they were issued perforated $9^{1}/_{2}$
and there is an extremely rare variety of the 2 kreuzer
yellow, which has been found in a tête-bêche pair.

In 1867 a series was issued showing the portrait of the
Emperor facing to the right, in a range of values from 2 to
50 kreuzer. Normally the 3 kreuzer was printed in green,
but a few examples have been found in red, the normal
colour of the 5 kreuzer. It is not known definitely whether
this error resulted from a complete sheet printed in the
wrong colour or from a cliché of the 3 kreuzer inadvertently
included in the 5 kreuzer plate. Most of the four or five

known examples of this error bear Hungarian postmarks. An example which was auctioned by H.R. Harmer in 1937 realized £ 225, a small proportion of its present value.

The 'Mercuries' were the first Austrian newspaper stamps and were so called because the design bears the portrait of the messenger of the gods. Rarest of them all is the 'Red Mercury' [figure 57], issued in 1856 for use as a 6 kreuzer stamp but reissued later for 0.6 kreuzer. It is a very rare stamp in unused condition, but even more so used, and only some seven examples are known in that state, all of them more or less defective. The same series includes the 'Rose Mercury' and the 'Yellow Mercury', both of which are rare but do not reach the extreme rarity of the red stamp. Another very rare Austrian newspaper stamp is the 1863 octagonal 1.05 kreuzer, lilac in a tête-bêche pair. The number of examples known is probably only two or three, and the Ferrary Collection contained the variety in the centre of an unused block of nine [figure 98].

One of the rarest stamps of Europe, of which only three examples are recorded, is the Baden 1851 9 kreuzer black on green. It is an error of colour, of which the circumstances of production are uncertain: as with the Austrian 3 kreuzer red error, it is not known whether the Baden 9 kreuzer (which should normally have been black on dull rose) occurred in a complete sheet or as one stamp in the sheets of the 6 kreuzer, the normal colour of which was indeed black on green.

The three known examples were all discovered at the same time in 1894 among the correspondence of a German nobleman. Two of them are still attached to the original letters; the third is on a small piece. One letter was in the Ferrary collection and later passed to A.H. Caspary; this realized $ 20,000 at the Caspary sale in April 1956. The other example on a letter is in the German Postal Museum at Frankfurt [figure 99]. The third stamp was in the Theodore Champion Collection.

98 Austria: newspaper stamps 1865
1.05 kreuzer centre stamps *tête-bêche* in block of six

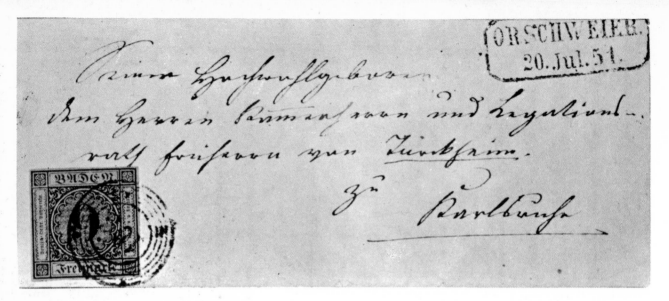

99 Baden: 1851 9 kreuzer black on green
error of colour used on cover

The 3 pfennig red of Saxony, 1850, [figure 58] is one of the most popular European rarities. Although on the score of numbers existing it is much commoner than many cheaper stamps, the constant demand for fine specimens keeps up the price. A unique block of four used is known [figure 100]. This stamp is known in a complete, though rather defective, sheet of twenty. The sheet was originally found by an English student on holiday in Dresden. One day he went for a boat trip along the Elbe as far as Koenigstein and visited the old castle of that name. In the baronial hall was a large fire-place and at the side two fire-screens in the shape of shields which could be moved up or down tall poles. 'The shields,' recounted the student many years afterwards, 'were covered with sheets of old 3 pfennig Saxon stamps, back to back' [figure 1].

Some time later the screens were seen by a Viennese stamp dealer who was successful in persuading the owner to allow the stamps to be removed. Most of them succumbed during the process, but this one surviving sheet was soaked off in its entirety and to this day bears evidence of the removal. The sheet was acquired by Ferrary and afterwards passed into the Burrus Collection. In 1966 this sheet realized 620,000 DM at an auction by H. C. Schwenn of Frankfurt, the highest price ever paid for a single item.

An error of colour occurred on the ¹/₂ neugroschen issued by Saxony in 1851 [figure 60]. The stamp was printed normally in black on grey paper, but a complete sheet of 120 stamps was struck by mistake on the pale blue paper of the 2 neugroschen. It is recorded that 63 of them were sold over the post office counter before the error was discovered. According to Michel's catalogue the remaining fifty-seven were sold by the post office to collectors in 1891 at the very modest price of 3 marks apiece. To judge by the very few examples of the error now known to exist, the figure of fifty-seven is probably too high. Ferrary had a block of ten, which was auctioned in the sixth sale of his collection and realized over £700, perhaps the price of a single specimen in 1966.

The early issues of France include varieties which, although not truly errors, are sometimes referred to as such. The printing plates were put together by Anatole Hulot, an eccentric who concealed his work under a cloak of secrecy and mystery. In some plates he inserted one or more clichés upside-down in relation to the others, and so created tête-bêche varieties. The reason why he did this has never been discovered. The varieties have been found on the 1849 10, 15, 20 and 25 centimes, the 1 franc in orange-vermilion (the so-called 'Vervelle') and in orange-brown [figure 101]; also on the 1853-61 80 centimes and 1 franc [figure 67], the 1862-71 20 and 80 centimes, the 1862-70 4 centimes, and 1870-76 10, 15, 20 and 25 centimes. Rarest of them all are the 1849 15 centimes and 1 franc orange-brown, of which only individual examples are known.

After Hulot died, a part-sheet of 1 franc stamps was found in an orange-vermilion shade without gum. The sheet was bought by Ernest Vervelle, a Parisian dealer, and ever since then stamps in this particular shade have been known by his name. He cut up the sheet and the solitary tête-bêche variety which it contained was cut into a block

100 Saxony: 1850 3 pfennig red, unique used block of four

101 France: 1849 1 franc: tête-bêche pair

102 France: 1869 5fr pair

103 France: 1869 5 francs with value omitted

of four, which was acquired by Ferrary. At the eleventh Ferrary sale this remarkable piece was sold for £2,700. The purchaser was Arthur Hind, and when his collection was sold in the depression days of 1934 the price slumped to £1,250. Since then it has not only regained, but far surpassed its former height.

In 1869 France issued her first 5 francs stamp. It was in a transverse design, showing the portrait of Napoleon III with the denomination on each side, and was printed in light grey. As the value was added at a second operation it is not very surprising that examples have been found with the value omitted [figure 103]. Only two such specimens are known used, both of them defective, and one unused. One used example was in the Ferrary Collection.

In 1859 a provisional government was set up in Modena, and as a result a series of new stamps was issued with a shield bearing the Cross of Savoy as the central feature. The values ranged from 5 to 80 centesimi. All are fairly scarce, but particularly rare is the 80c in used condition. There was little demand for this denomination; when the stamps were withdrawn there were considerable remainders that were sold on the collectors' market. Consequently, unused examples are still obtainable at a comparatively moderate figure; used are 200 times as costly.

Much less expensive are the two blue newspaper stamps issued by Naples in 1860, known to philatelists as the 'Trinacria' and 'Savoy Cross'. Both were sold at half a tornese each. The 'Trinacria', bearing the arms of the Bourbons, was issued in November and had been in use for only a very short time when Garibaldi's armies conquered Naples. Thereupon the printing plate was altered and a Savoy Cross substituted in the centre of each design [figures 65, 66].

The stamps were popular even among the early collectors and the search for specimens was keen. There is a tale that a collector at Naples had an artist friend who had subscribed to several papers at the time when these stamps were cur-

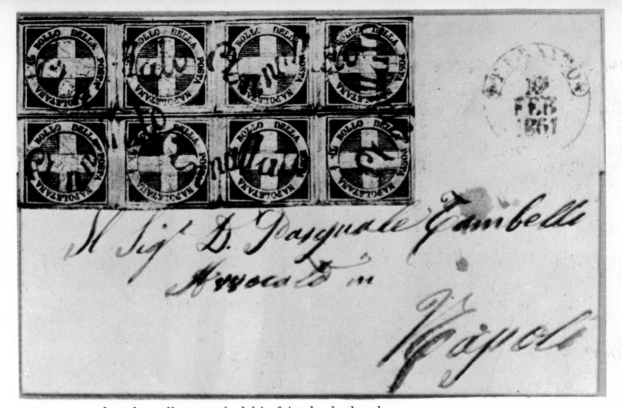

rent; so one day the collector asked his friend whether he had kept any of the old papers, in the hope that there might still be some stamps affixed to them. The artist, shook his head, then added, to the collector's delight, that the stamps had been removed, because they were printed in such a pretty blue colour, and he had stuck them all over the top of a round table which stood in his studio. 'But some time ago, I had the table put into the store-room,' said the artist.

He called his maid and asked her to bring down the stamp-covered table. She hesitated, blushed, and at last stammered out, 'The round table, Sir – I quite forgot to tell you that it happened this way. It had been so long in the dust and had been so often rubbed over that it had become quite discoloured, and so dirty, that I tried, by washing it a little, to make it clean again. I therefore took a little soft soap and rubbed it gently with a fine sponge, but although I went to work very softly, I soon discovered, but unfortunate-

104 Naples: 1860, a block of eight of the Savoy Cross used on cover

105 Neapolitan Provinces: ¹/₂ tornese black error of colour

ly too late, that the paper was working into lumps, so I thought it would be best, as I could do no better, to clean it off altogether, and now the wood is quite plain, as it was originally, and I think it looks nicer like that.'

Like most issues of the Italian states, the 'Trinacria' and the 'Savoy Cross' have increased in value very substantially in recent years. This applies particularly to unused examples.

Much rarer than either of those stamps is the half grano of Sicily printed in cobalt instead of its normal orange. Only two specimens of this error are known to collectors. One was included in the collection formed by Prince Doria Pamphilj, and when sold by H. R. Harmer in 1963 realized £5,000.

The Neapolitan provinces issued only one series of stamps, ranging from ¹/₂ tornese to 50 grana, in 1861. All are in the same design, showing in the centre an embossed head of Victor Emmanuel II, and the various denominations differ only in colour and the value in words at the foot. Two errors of colour occurred in this series and both are very rare. The ¹/₂ tornese [figure 105] and the 2 grana have been found printed in black instead of green and blue respectively. The few known specimens of the ¹/₂ tornese all bear the postmark of Roccagloriosa, and the 2 grana, which is even rarer, was used at Potenza.

Extremely rare is the tête-bêche variety which can be found on the 15 centesimi of Parma's 1852 issue. The number of pairs in existence showing this variety seems to be unrecorded, but there was one in the Ferrary Collection and it fetched the incredibly low price of £97 at the ninth sale. The present value would run well into the thousands.

Undoubtedly one of Europe's most famous rarities is the Tuscany 3 lire buff of 1860 [figure 78]. This stamp was the top value in a set of seven issued by the provisional government after Garibaldi's victory, and shows the arms of Savoy instead of those of the former Grand Duke Leopold II.

The 3 lire was not always rare, and most of the surviving specimens owe their existence to an Englishman whose initials were G. A. W. He, incidentally, used to collect stamps in an odd way, since he cut adhesive and envelope stamps to shape, put all specimens of one country together and entrusted their arrangement to an artist, who made many kinds of combinations of them without paying any regard to the chronology of issues. This early collector apparently had extensive correspondence with Tuscany at the time when the 3 lire stamp was in use, and he supplied a quantity of his duplicates of this value to the Belgian dealer J. B. Moëns at 50 centimes each; Moëns was pleased to resell them at 75 centimes, but the demand was considerable and the modest price very soon began to rise, a process which has continued ever since. As the Tuscan stamps were printed very close to one another in the sheet, they were often cut into when being separated, so that most of the known examples of the 3 lire are not in perfect condition.

The first stamps issued in Rumania appeared in 1858. In those days the Danubian principalities had not been merged into what later became Rumania, and Moldavia was the first principality to have its own stamps. They were primitive, hand-stamped impressions with a bull's head in the centre, and they are known to philatelists as the 'Moldavian Bulls'.

The four values were 27 parales, black on rose paper (of which 6,000 were printed), 54p blue on green (of which there were 10,000), 81p blue on pale blue (2,000) and 108p blue on pink (6,000) [figures 80 and 81]. From these figures it will be gathered that none of these stamps is common, and their rarity has been increased by the fact that the remainders of all values were destroyed some years after the stamps went out of use.

The rarest single stamp is the 81p, but the 27p exists in a tête-bêche pair, and this is the rarest of them all. It is on record that Dr J. A. Legrand, a noted pioneer philatelist, bought an 81p for the equivalent of 2s 6d in the eighteen-sixties; in 1897 this stamp was sold for £500.

Ferrary, whose name has appeared so often in these pages,

106 Dr Jacques Amable Legrand, a noted pioneer philatelist

107 Philipp la Renotière von Ferrary, whose collection contained numerous rarities described and illustrated in this book

108 Spain: 1851 2 reales blue in pair with 6 reales

was famous for his accumulation of rarities, and one of the rarest items he ever obtained was the Spanish 2 reales blue of 1851 [figure 68]. This stamp was an error: it should have been printed in red, but was produced when a cliché of the 2 reales was accidentally inserted in the plate of the 6 reales of the same issue.

The Ferrary collection contained two of the errors, one being unused and the other used in a pair with a normal 6 reales [figure 108]. This pair has an interesting history. In 1899 a block of either fourteen or eighteen blue stamps of the 1851 issue was offered to A. Galvez, the Madrid dealer, but as the price asked was too high he refused to buy the block. It was then offered to one of his competitors and a deal resulted. The purchaser gave the stamps to a woman employee with instructions to cut up the block into single specimens which would sell more easily. She began dividing the stamps and had reached the last pair when she noticed that the upper stamp was inscribed 'dos' (two) and the lower stamp 'seis' (six). She pointed out this curiosity to her employer, and the dealer was delighted with the discovery. Some time afterwards the pair was bought by Ferrary, and in later years by King Carol of Rumania; in 1950 it was acquired by René Berlingin together with several other rarities. There is an unused example of this error in the Tapling collection.

The 5 reales of the same Spanish issue, normally printed in rose, exists in chocolate brown, but this error is much less rare than that of the 2 reales.

A popular rarity among philatelists occurs in the 1872 issue of Sweden. The central feature of the design of every stamp in this series consists of the figures of value enclosed in a circular frame containing their equivalent in words. The stamps remained in use for some years, and in 1879, when a new printing was about to begin, it was discovered that one cliché in the plate of the 20 öre had become damaged. No substitute cliché of that denomination was available, so the difficulty was overcome by adapting a 30 öre cliché: The figures '30' were excised and '20' inserted in their place. The cliché was then fitted into position and printing began; 6,000 sheets were produced.

Nearly 1,600 of them had been distributed to post offices when somebody discovered that there was an error on the substituted cliché. Although the figures were '20', the value in words was thirty (*tretio*) [figure 69]. Presumably the workman who altered the cliché had forgotten to change the wording! As soon as the mistake was discovered, the Post Office ordered their withdrawal, but only about 600 were recovered, the remaining 1,000 having already been sold.

The variety has become known to philatelists as the 'Tretio error', and its increasing popularity has led to a vast increase in price over the years. There is a record of £5 5s having been paid for a used example in 1892; seventy-four years later the price had reached about £250.

Three years after the world's first adhesive postage stamps appeared in Great Britain, the Swiss canton of Zürich issued two stamps: one of 4 and other of 6 rappen value [figure 109]. The 4 rappen was for local postage, and the 6 rappen for postage within neighbouring cantons. Neither value is easy to find, but the 4 is particularly rare. This denomination is known bisected and used together with a whole stamp to make up the 6 rappen rate. A letter bearing such a bisect is one of the rarest Swiss items.

109 Switzerland: the Zürich 4 rappen and 6 rappen strips showing the five transfer types

Later in 1843 the canton of Geneva issued its first stamp. It was an unusual issue, a stamp in two parts, each valued at 5 centimes, for local use, and with a label extending across the top inscribed 10 centimes, to show that if both stamps were used together, they would cover the cantonal postage [figure 61]. The 'Double Geneva', as, collectors call it, is very rare, and fine examples always realize high prices. Curiously, the fact that each half of the stamps was inscribed 5 centimes, and the label across the top was inscribed 10 centimes, led one of the leading early philatelists to think that the 'Double Geneva' was bogus. He could not reconcile the differing denominations with a genuine issue. He was eventually convinced, however, when he saw examples used on letters. A fine unused block of 6 in the Burrus Collection realized 475,000 Swiss francs (£43,500) in 1964.

In 1845 the best-looking early Swiss stamp appeared. It was issued at Basle and had as its central feature a white dove in flight with a letter in its beak. Philatelists dubbed

110 Reunion: 1852 15c black on bluish and 30c black on bluish used on cover to France

the stamp the 'Basle Dove' [figure 59]. It is notable as being the first stamp ever to be printed in three colours: red, black and blue on an uncoloured ground. Examples are rare, but some fine pieces exist. An unused block of fifteen was discovered about 1909, when part of an archive office at Basle was being redecorated and the stamps were found in a slit in the wallpaper above a mantelpiece. Apparently they had been put there many years earlier, and then forgotten, by a citizen of Basle who had bought a sheet while the stamps were in use. The block was bought by Henry J. Duveen and later passed into the Alfred F. Lichtenstein Collection.

After Geneva's original issue the same canton issued two other stamps between 1849 and 1850. Both were in the same design, showing the Swiss cross in the centre, and were printed in black and red. The 5 centimes of this issue is not very rare, but the 4 centimes certainly is. A used pair on a small piece of letter which was in the Burrus Collection realized 31,000 Swiss francs (about £2,500) at the sale in 1964.

111 Finland: 1856 10 kop rose, an unused block exhibiting three tête-bêche pairs

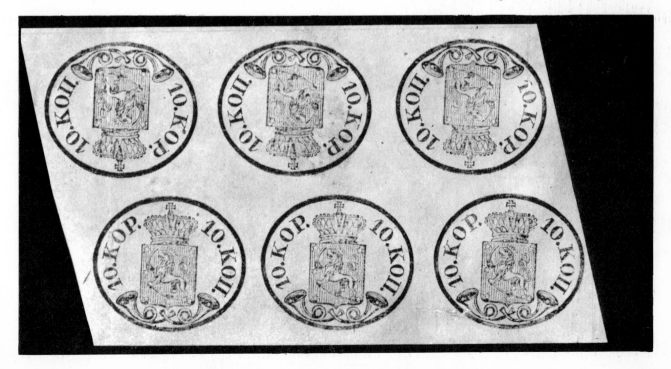

CHAPTER FIVE

American rarities

THE UNITED STATES OF AMERICA has offered a wide choice in the field of rarities. The first official issue of the US Post Office did not appear until 1847, but in the year or two before then a number of postmasters issued their own stamps for use on mail, and some of these issues include what have become the world's greatest rarities.

Daniel Bryan, Postmaster of Alexandria, at that time in the District of Columbia but now in Virginia, issued some crude circular stamps about 1846. The design was simple: 'Alexandria' around the upper part, 'Post Office' around the lower part, with 'Paid 5' in the centre, the whole being enclosed in a circular frame of rosettes. The stamps were printed on buff [figure 114, 115] and also on blue paper. Only six of the first colour have been recorded, and there is a solitary specimen of the second.

The circumstances surrounding the discovery of the Alexandria 'Blue Boy', as it is known, are romantic. Towards the end of 1847 James Wallace Hooff was courting Jannett Brown, who was his second cousin. They both lived in Alexandria, but at the relevant time she was on a visit to relatives at Richmond, Virginia. The lovers corresponded with each other and one November day he wrote her a budget of friendly family news, referring to their secret betrothal, and as they did not want that to be disclosed at the

114 USA: postmasters' stamps, Alexandria 1846 5c black on buff

112 (*opposite left*) USA: St Louis Bears reconstruction of plate in first state

113 (*opposite right*) USA: St Louis Bears 20 cents

79

time, he added at the end: 'Burn this letter'. Fortunately she did not do so, because he had stuck on the letter one of the Alexandria stamps then in use. In due course James and Jannett were married and the ceremony took place at her home, at 517, Prince Street, Alexandria, where later they were to spend the rest of their lives. Jannett died in 1879.

In 1907, while going through some old correspondence, her daughter, Mrs. Fawcett, came across a bundle of her mother's old love letters, and was struck by the curious appearance of the stamp on the letter which her mother had not burnt as instructed. Mrs. Fawcett knew nothing about stamps, but she showed the letter to a friend who was a stamp collector, and he considered that the stamp was valuable, suggesting that she should write to a stamp dealer and tell him of the discovery. The dealer replied at once, evincing interest, and later offered $ 3,000 for the stamp. Had he taken the first train to Alexandria no doubt he could have bought this rarity, but as it was it passed into the collection of George H. Worthington for the same amount. In later years it changed hands more than once and about 1922 passed into the Caspary collection. At H. R. Harmer's first

115 USA: Alexandria on cover
116 USA: the unique Boscawen stamp on cover

Caspary sale in 1955 the letter realized $10,000. The letter came on the market again in February 1967, when, at Robert A. Siegel's first sale of the Josiah K. Lilly collection, it sold for $18,500.

The Caspary collection contained also three of the buff stamps, and these remained in America after the sales.

Two other US Postmasters' provisionals, the 'Boscawen' [figure 116] and the 'Lockport', are unique. The 'Boscawen' is as crude as could be, consisting of just the legend 'Paid 5 Cents' hand stamped on a rectangular piece of rather crumpled paper. The stamp is affixed to a letter addressed to Concord, NH, and was discovered in 1865 by a stamp collector who had obtained it from an employee in the General Post Office at Washington, DC. Although the collector had never seen such a stamp before, he did not doubt that it was genuine because of its source. For twenty-nine years he kept it and then, in February 1894, he offered it, together with some other stamps, to a well-known American philatelist, Hiram E. Deats. Deats, too, had never seen a similar specimen, but when he showed the letter to a New York dealer, the dealer became excited and rather downhearted, because he had found a similar stamp and had then lost it.

In 1912 Deats sold part of his collection, including the 'Boscawen', to W. H. Colson, the well-known dealer, who exchanged the letter with Ferrary for a 2d 'Post Office' Mauritius. At the third Ferrary sale in 1922 the 'Boscawen' was bought by Arthur Hind for about £2,500, but eleven years later the envelope fetched a mere $5,000 at the Hind sale. This relatively low price was due to the fact that the Hind collection was auctioned when the market was at a low ebb because of the depression. In November 1964 the envelope figured in Robert A. Siegel's sale, when the price shot up to $23,000, the purchasers being the New Orleans dealers Raymond H. Weill & Co.

The 'Lockport' is an oval impression struck in red on buff affixed to a letter [figure 117]. The design is a crude as the

117 USA: the Lockport stamp on cover

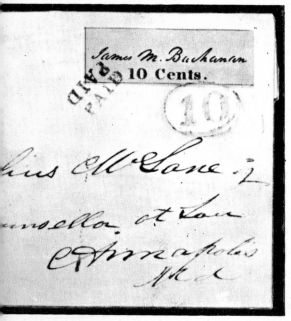

118, 119 USA: postmasters' stamps, Baltimore 1846 10c black on cover

'Boscawen' and the inscription reads 'Paid' in the centre, with 'Lockport' round the upper part and 'N.Y.' round the lower part of the oval, with a figure 5 added in manuscript in the centre. The circumstances of the stamp's issue have never been discovered. At the time when it appeared, the Lockport Postmaster was Colonel H. W. Scovell, and although it is thought that the stamp was issued on his authority, there is no proof that this was the case.

The letter bearing the stamp was found near the end of the nineteenth century by an enthusiastic philatelist who was searching through old letters in the files of a Lockport firm. He thought little of this crude specimen, and after keeping it for a year or so he offered it to the Scott Stamp and Coin Company, of New York. They took the Lockport in exchange for some other stamps, and later sold it to Ferrary. At the third Ferrary sale Arthur Hind bought the letter for £1,835, but again it showed a substantial loss when sold at the auctions of his collection in 1933, the price being only $2,500. The purchaser was W. H. Colson, and from him the 'Lockport' passed into the Caspary collection. At the Caspary sales this item realized $5,500.

Another US Postmaster to issue his own stamps in the year or two before the first government issues appeared was James Madison Buchanan, Postmaster of Baltimore. His stamps were rather better looking than some, and consisted of a reproduction of his signature, with the value neatly printed beneath it and enclosed in a rectangular frame. There were two denominations, 5 and 10 cents, and both exist on white or bluish paper. The 10 cents is infinitely rarer than the lower denomination, and no more than seven examples have been recorded.

Although the stamps had been issued in 1846, twenty-nine years passed before they became known to collectors, and then only the 5 cents was recorded. The 10 cents did not turn up until 1895, when a damaged specimen was discovered. The discovery was not given any publicity. Early the following year an American dealer put an advertisement in a Washington theatre programme, offering to buy old stamps and stating that he would pay $ 100 each for the 5 cents of Baltimore, or much more for the 10 cents. Not long afterwards he was visited by an old lady, dressed in black. She said she had read the advertisement and had come to ask whether he really would pay $ 100 for a Baltimore 5 cents stamp. When he assured her that he would, she asked how much he would pay for a 10 cents.

He smiled and replied that it did not matter anyway, because no stamps of that value had been found, but when she persisted with her enquiry, he said that it would depend on whether one could find a very wealthy collector to buy such a stamp. At this she opened her handbag and took out a perfect example of the 10 cents on white paper still attached to the letter it had franked [figure 118, 119].

The dealer was astounded and said that he could not make up his mind at once, but that if she would leave the letter with him for a few days, he would make an offer for it. Later that week he agreed to sell the letter for a 10% commission, and soon afterwards this rarity passed into the Ferrary collection for $ 3,300. Another example of the stamp, used on a letter addressed to London, was included in Robert A. Siegel's auction in November 1964 and realized $ 9,000.

The Postmaster of Millbury, Mass., Colonel A. H. Waters, was another to issue his own stamps in 1846. He used an attractive design showing the head of George Washington enclosed in a circular frame inscribed 'Post Office Paid 5 Cts' [figure 120]. The stamps were somewhat crudely engraved on wood and were printed, one at a time, on a handpress in Boston. The first example was found in a bound volume of letters at the library of the American Antiquarian Society in Worcester, Mass., and several others have been discovered since then, one being unused with full gum. That specimen once graced the Ferrary Collection; years later it

120 USA: the Millbury stamp on cover

121 USA: postmasters' stamps, Brattleboro 1846 5c on cover

122 USA: the New Haven stamp

passed to Josiah K. Lilly and at the first sale of his collection in 1967 it fetched $34,000.

In 1846 the Postmaster of Brattleboro, Vermont, was Frederick N. Palmer, and he issued a neat little stamp, printed in black on buff paper, inscribed with the name of the town at the top, '5 cents' at the foot, and his initials in a panel in the centre. As was the case with other postmasters of the period, Palmer's income was increased in proportion to the number of prepaid letters passing through his hands, and he issued his stamp in the expectation that its use would increase his earnings.

Most of the US Postmasters' stamps were adhesive, but two were struck on envelopes. One of these was the Annapolis, Maryland, issue; the other was used at New Haven, Connecticut.

The Annapolis shows the American eagle in the centre of a circle, with 'Post Office, Annapolis, Md.' around a circular frame, and it is said to have been used on the authority of Martin F. Revell, who was Postmaster in 1846. The impression was struck intaglio in red. Only some three examples are known. The New Haven was issued under the authority of E. A. Mitchell, the Postmaster. The stamp is an upright rectangle with scalloped corners, and the inscription reads 'Post Office New Haven, Ct. 5 Paid', with the Postmaster's signature at the foot, followed by the letters 'P. M.' [figure 122]. The stamp was struck in red or blue on letters handed in for transmission, and so exists on different papers according to whatever colour the envelope was. Fewer than half a dozen examples have been found. A letter bearing an impression in red realized $23,000 at the first sale of the J. K. Lilley collection in 1967.

The 'St Louis Bears', so called because the design shows the arms of St Louis, with two bears as supporters, were first issued in November 1845 under the authority of John M. Wimer, the Postmaster. There were three denominations, 5, 10 and 20 cents, all printed in black on greenish-grey paper, and the printing plate contained six stamps, at first three each of the 5 and 10 cent [figure 112], but later one 5, three 10 and two 20 cents stamps [figure 113]. Later printings were on grey-lilac paper, and there was a final printing on bluish-grey paper, but for that printing the plate was restored to its original arrangement and did not contain any of the 20 cents. All these stamps are rare, particularly the top value.

There were two great finds of 'St Louis Bears', one in 1895, and the other in 1912. The first was made by a Negro porter who was told to clear out the cellars at the Court House in Louisville, Kentucky, and to burn all the accumulated bundles of papers lying there. After lighting the furnace, he was shovelling the bundles into it when one came adrift and he noticed that the papers had unusual stamps on them. Putting some on one side he later showed them to two caretakers in the building and they treated him to a drink in exchange for the stamps. The following day the caretakers went down to the cellar and found many more stamps. By carefully disposing of their find, they made, it is said, about $20,000. The second find was made at Philadelphia, when a change in the partnership of a banking firm led to the clearing out of some of the firm's old papers and letters. They were sold for $50 to a paper pulping company, and when they were sorted, it was found that many letters bore St Louis stamps. At the time it was stated that altogether there were 105 specimens, all bought by a syndicate of New York stamp dealers for around $100,000, but informed opinion is that there were some twenty-eight of the 10 cents and six of the 20 cents and that the contemporary figures were grossly exaggerated.

In 1869 the United States Post Office Department issued its first bi-coloured stamps. They were the highest four values in a series of ten. The 15 cents, depicting the landing of Columbus after Vanderlyn's painting in the Capitol at Washington, the 24 cents, showing the Declaration of Inde-

123 USA: 1869 15 cents with inverted centre
124 USA: 1869 24 cents with inverted centre
125 USA: 1869 30 cents with inverted flags

pendence, from Turnbull's painting, and the 30 cents, which shows the Stars and Stripes and a shield, have all been found with the centres inverted [figures 123, 124, 125].

The first of these errors was discovered by a Government agent named Anthony, who found among his supply a complete sheet of the 15 cents with inverted centres. One stamp was sold and passed into a collection, but the remaining ninety-nine were returned by Anthony to a post office, presumably for destruction. Even in those early days the discovery was soon noised abroad, and philatelists began searching for the errors. J. W. Scott, the well-known dealer, went through his own stock of the 15 cents and found several examples of the error, which he recorded for the first time in the *American Journal of Philately* for 20 December 1870, and at the same time he stated that the 24 cents existed in a similar state. Several years later the 30 cents with inverted flags was discovered.

The finest known piece in this group is a used block of the 24 cents which was found at Liverpool towards the end of the nineteenth century. The block was bought by a local dealer and was sold for a mere £5 to a well-known New York collector. After changing hands several times, the block was acquired by William H. Crocker, of San Francisco, and at Harmer, Rooke & Co.'s sale of his collection in 1938 this choice item realized £2,500, the purchaser being a dealer acting on behalf of E. B. Martin. A used example of the 30 cents with inverted flags realized £650 and went to the same bidder.

In unused condition all three errors are extreme rarities, and altogether only eight specimens in that condition have been recorded, two each of the 15 and 24 cents, and four of the 30 cents.

The Columbian Exposition at Chicago in 1893 was made the occasion of an issue of commemorative stamps showing scenes from the life of Columbus. The 4 cents of this series, normally printed in ultramarine, has been found in deep

126 USA: 1901 1c Pan-American invert

blue, the colour of the 1 cent. Whether this was a true error of colour or a colour trial issued by mistake is not known, but examples have been found used and unused. In unused condition they are specially valuable.

A set of five stamps, issued in 1901 for the Pan-American Exhibition at Buffalo, provides three examples of inverted centres, all of them rare. They occur on the 1 cent depicting a lake steamer [figure 126], the 2 cents showing a railway train, and the 4 cents with an early automobile as its central feature. The first error to be discovered was on the 2 cents; F.W. Davis was supplied with a sheet of fifty of these stamps, and saw to his delight that they all had the centres inverted. Davis was a stamp collector and he decided to dispose of most of the stamps as quickly as possible, because he feared that many more such errors might exist, which would seriously affect the price. He managed to sell most of them, according to John W. Nicklin in *Fabulous Stamps*, at prices ranging between $2 and $75 each. Another find of ten stamps was made by a man who was not a philatelist and who used three of them on letters before noticing the error. He then wrote to the Bureau of Engraving and Printing, complaining about the error, and asking whether the stamps were valid for postage. The Director replied stating that the stamps had been issued by mistake, but that they were perfectly good for postal use. By the time the letter arrived the purchaser had discovered his good fortune and sold the balance of his find for what was stated in the contemporary philatelic press to have been 'a pretty good price'.

News of the existence of errors on the 2 cents spread all over the country and people began a hectic search for 'Pan-American Inverts'. The next find was a sheet of the 4 cents, but this was not issued at a post office and was discovered at the Bureau of Engraving and Printing. The stamps were to be destroyed, but a few examples were rescued by the Third Assistant Postmaster General, and subsequently they came

127 USA: Confederate States: the crude stamp of Grove Hill

128 (*opposite above*) Transvaal: 1869
1s tête-bêche pair

129 (*below*) Uruguay: 1858 180 centesimos in
tête bêche pair

into the hands of philatelists. Most of these stamps were overprinted 'Specimen'.

During the American Civil War supplies of US postage stamps were withheld from the Confederate States, and indeed, where stocks of existing issues were captured by the Southern Armies, those stamps were demonetized by the Northern postal authorities and replaced by other stamps. The Confederates made arrangements for the printing of their own stamps, some of which were produced and issued under the authority of local postmasters.

Rarest of them is the stamp of Mount Lebanon, Louisiana, of which just one example has ever been found. It is a curious stamp, engraved in reverse, so that all the inscriptions read backwards. It is printed in red-brown, and is still affixed to the envelope which it franked. This unique item, at one time in the Ferrary Collection, later passed to A. H. Caspary, and at the sale of his stamps in March 1956 it realized $5,500.

Not quite as rare, but a stamp of which probably not more than three exist, is the issue of Grove Hill, Alabama. It was very crudely engraved on wood and printed in black [figure 127]. Two examples, both used on letters, were in the Caspary Collection, one realizing $7,000, and the other no more than $2,500, because, unlike its more expensive counterpart, it had been cancelled by pen and not with a postmark.

After Great Britain had issued the world's first adhesive postage stamps in 1840 the idea spread very gradually to other countries, and in 1843 Brazil followed the example. Although in those days Brazil had an Emperor, she decided not to put his portrait on her postage stamps. Instead the design consisted mainly of large ornamental figures of value against an engine-turned background. The shape of the stamps and their appearance led to their becoming known as 'Bulls' Eyes'. They were of three denominations: 30, 60 and 90 reis, all printed in black. The printing plates at first consisted of fifty-four impressions, three panes of eighteen

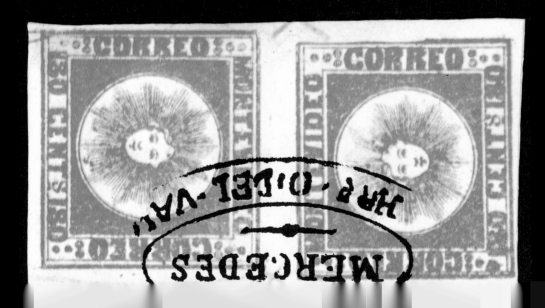

stamps of each value. Usually the panes were separated before being issued, but in at least one case this seems not to have been done, and there is in existence a unique vertical strip of three, consisting of two of the 30 reis and one of the 60 reis [figure 130]. At one time this was in the C. Lathrop Pack collection, and later passed into another well-known collection before being sold at auction in London in 1963 for £8,250.

No less than those in Brazil, the early issues of Uruguay include some rarities. The stamps are known as the 'Montevideo Suns', because the central feature of the design is a cherubic face surrounded by rays. The first issue of 1856 is very scarce, but not nearly as rare as varieties of the 1856 issue, where the 120 centesimos and 180 centesimos have been found in tête-bêche pairs [figure 129]. The stamps were lithographed in sheets of seventy-eight and one design in each sheet was inverted; a tête-bêche pair of the 120c is in the Tapling collection, and another in the collection of Mrs Louise Dale, of New York.

The 240 centesimos of this issue was printed in sheets of 204, and seven stamp-sized spaces were left blank. The blank spaces occurred at regular intervals in the sheet and may have been due to the removal of defective transfers when the stone was built up. A complete sheet was in existence at one time, but in 1910 it was bought by a London firm of dealers who failed to find a purchaser at the

130 Brazil: 1843 vertical strip of three showing one 60 reis se-tenant with two 30 reis

131 *(right)* Mexico: 1921 10 centavos with inverted centre

price then asked (£1,650), so they were obliged to cut it up in order to sell it.

The same issue includes a much disputed error of colour on the 180c. Normally this stamp was printed in green, but two examples have been found in the dull red of the 240c. It was believed at one time that the 'error' was a colour changeling, but examination of a specimen in the Ferrary Collection by eminent philatelists led them to pronounce it as genuine.

In 1892 Mexico issued a series of stamps in values ranging from 1 centavo to 10 pesos. The highest two values, the 5 and 10 pesos, were in a design showing the portrait of Hidalgo, and in this case both were printed in blue-green instead of the blue which had been used for the stamps in 1884. Both these varieties of colour are rare, particularly in unused condition. There is another much rarer Mexican stamp, however, issued in 1921. It is the 10 centavos commemorative, showing the meeting between Iturbide and Guerrero, with the central part of the design inverted. Only two or three examples of this error are known to exist, one of which was in the collection of Irving I. Ingraham, through whose kindness it is illustrated [figure 131].

132 *(overleaf left)* Trinidad: the 'Lady McLeod' on part of cover

133 *(overleaf right)* South Australia: 1879 4d deep ultramarine surcharge omitted

THIS SPACE FOR MESSAGE

Good Birthday
Greetings.
Via "AERIAL Post"
"ZACH"
Dallas. Oct. 17. 1911
Texas

25 CENTS 25
RODGERS AERIAL POST
VIN
VIN FIZ FLYER
25 CENTS 25

U.S. POSTAGE
ONE CENT

WACO
OCT 20
1-30P
19   1
TEXAS

Miss MARGHRETTA L. PIERCE
#314 West 99 Th Street
New York
"BUCKINGHAM Court." N.Y.

CHAPTER SIX

Rarities of the Air

THE STAMPS issued for franking mail carried on pioneer long-distance flights have a charm all their own; the endurance and privations of the early fliers, reflected in the stamps, has contributed, as much as their actual rarity, towards the great demand for them.

Among the earliest issues in this group is the Newfoundland 'Hawker'. No important long-distance flights had been made before the First World War, and several people took up the challenge soon after the end of the war when the *Daily Mail* offered a prize of £10,000 to the first airman flying across the Atlantic Ocean in seventy-two hours or less. Among them were George Hawker and Lt-Cmdr Kenneth Mackenzie Grieve, who were to attempt the flight in a Sopwith biplane, powered by one 360 hp Rolls-Royce engine. They arrived at St John's, Newfoundland, towards the end of March 1919 and made preparations to set out on 16 April, day of the full moon.

J.A. Robinson, Postmaster-General of Newfoundland, made arrangements for the carriage of mail on the flight, and he prepared a provisional issue of stamps for use on the mail by overprinting the then current 3 cents brown of Newfoundland's 'Caribou' issue with the five-line inscription 'First Trans-Atlantic Air Post, April, 1919' [figure 134a]. Only 200 of these provisionals were produced, at the offices of the *Royal Gazette*.

Bad weather delayed the start of the flight for a month,

134a Newfoundland: 1919, a pair of the Hawker

134 (*opposite*) USA: 1911 Vin Fiz stamp on card

135 (*overleaf left*) Australia: 1920 Ross Smith Vignette used on cover

136 (*overleaf right*) Newfoundland: 1919 a Raynham-Morgan cover

FIRST
AERIAL POST

ENGLAND

FIRST AERIAL MAIL
RECEIVED
26 FEB 1920
GREAT BRITAIN TO AUSTRALIA

FIRST AERIAL MAIL
RECEIVED
26 FEB 1920
GREAT BRITAIN TO AUSTRALIA

Do Mrs Grace Carter

Denblane

Larken Street

Roseville

North Shore Line

Sydney N.S.W

Australia

Per Aeroplane "Raymor"
Newfoundland to Britain
Kindness of Major Morgan
and Fred Raynham Esq.

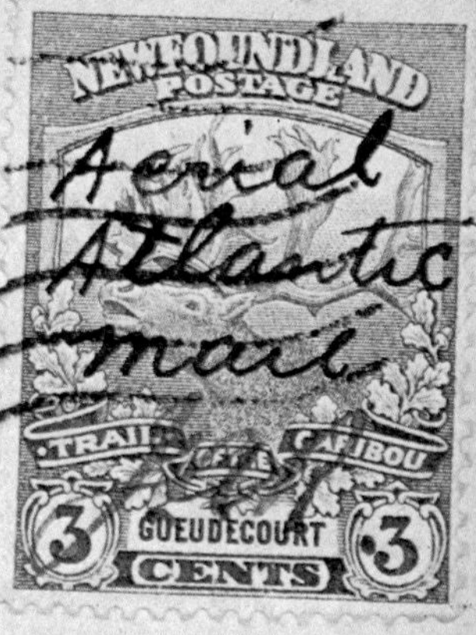
NEWFOUNDLAND
POSTAGE
Aerial
Atlantic
Mail
TRAIL OF THE CARIBOU
GUEUDECOURT
3
CENTS
3

ST JOHN'S, NFLD.
APR 19
4 PM
1919

Mr. James S. Ayre,
c/o J J Langley Ltd
Bank Chambers,
Cook St.
Liverpool.
England

From
F W Ayre.

137 Newfoundland: 1919, the Martinsyde

and it was not until 18 May that the machine was airborne, rising over St John's and heading for Ireland. Weather conditions deteriorated during the flight and after a series of hair-raising experiences the fliers decided that they could not complete their intended journey. Their only hope of survival rested in their sighting a ship which might rescue them if they came down sufficiently near it in the Atlantic. On 19 May they caught sight of a Danish tramp steamer, came down in a rough sea and were successfully taken off the plane, which at the time could not be salvaged.

Hawker and Grieve were brought to England and some time afterwards their machine was towed to Falmouth by an American vessel. Although the mail bags and their contents had suffered through immersion in the sea, it was possible to deliver the letters.

Only ninety-five stamps had been used on mail, and of the others eighteen were damaged and destroyed, eleven unused examples went as presentation copies, one into the Royal Collection, and the remaining seventy-six were sold at $25 each in aid of the Permanent Marine Disaster Fund. Since then the 'Hawker' has seen a remarkable rise in price, and at Harmer's sale of the Louise S. Hoffman Collection in March 1966 an unused example was sold for $4,200, another specimen used on a cover fetching the same amount.

Waiting at Newfoundland at the same time as Hawker and Grieve were John Alcock and Arthur Whitten Brown with a Vickers-Vimy biplane. In June 1919 they flew across the Atlantic in sixteen hours twenty minutes, and landed at Clifton, Ireland. They were the first men ever to fly the Atlantic in a heavier-than-air machine, and accordingly won the £10,000 prize. The 15 cents red of the 1897 Cabot issue of Newfoundland was overprinted with the legend 'Trans-Atlantic Air Post, 1919. One Dollar'. This stamp in itself is not at all rare, but used on a cover carried by Alcock and Brown it is a desirable item.

Another team waiting at Newfoundland for an opportunity to take off consisted of Captain Fred Raynham and Major Morgan, who had a Martinsyde plane. A very small number of 'Caribou' stamps, ranging between 1 and 24 cents, was overprinted for this flight, but not issued, and ten copies of the 3 cents 'Caribou' were inscribed in manuscript with 'Aerial Atlantic Mail' and initialled 'J.A.R.' by the Postmaster-General. These stamps were used on letters, which were, in fact, never flown, because the plane crashed on taking off. Some of the mail was taken to London by sea and eventually delivered in January 1920. The few surviving letters invariably fetch high prices, and one of these items was sold for $7,250 at the Hoffman sale.

In May 1927 the Marquis Francesco de Pinedo attempted to fly non-stop from Newfoundland to Rome, but before he reached his destination his sea-plane developed engine trouble and he came down in the water. He was rescued and towed to the Azores, and eventually completed the flight by 1 June. For this flight the 60 cents of the Cabot set was overprinted in red with 'Air Mail de Pinedo, 1927' [figure 138]. No more than 300 stamps were overprinted in this manner, most of which were used on mail. In unused condition the stamp is a great rarity and an example in the Hoffman collection realized $9,250. Another specimen used on a cover signed by De Pinedo achieved $4,750 in the sale.

In October 1930 the monoplane 'Columbia', piloted by Captain J. Erroll Boyd and Lt H.P. Connor, left Newfoundland and flew non-stop to Croydon, England. For this flight the 36 cents 'Caribou' stamp was overprinted 'Trans-Atlantic Air Mail By B.M. "Columbia" September 1930 Fifty Cents' [figure 143, 144]. The total printing in this case, too, was 300, and sales were restricted to a solitary stamp to each purchaser. About 150 were used and most of the remaining mint examples are still in existence, one of them fetching $1,600 at the Hoffman sale.

In July 1933 General Balbo's squadron of Italian sea-planes made the return flight from Chicago to Rome, and for

138 Newfoundland: 1927 the De Pinedo stamp (Note: the overprint shows only faintly in this illustration)

139 (overleaf above left) Italy: Balbo triptyches

140 (below left) USA: 1877 Buffalo Balloon stamp on cover

141 (right) Switzerland: Geneva 1849 4c

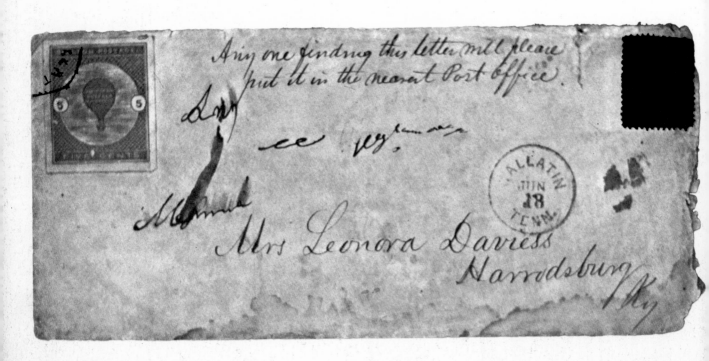

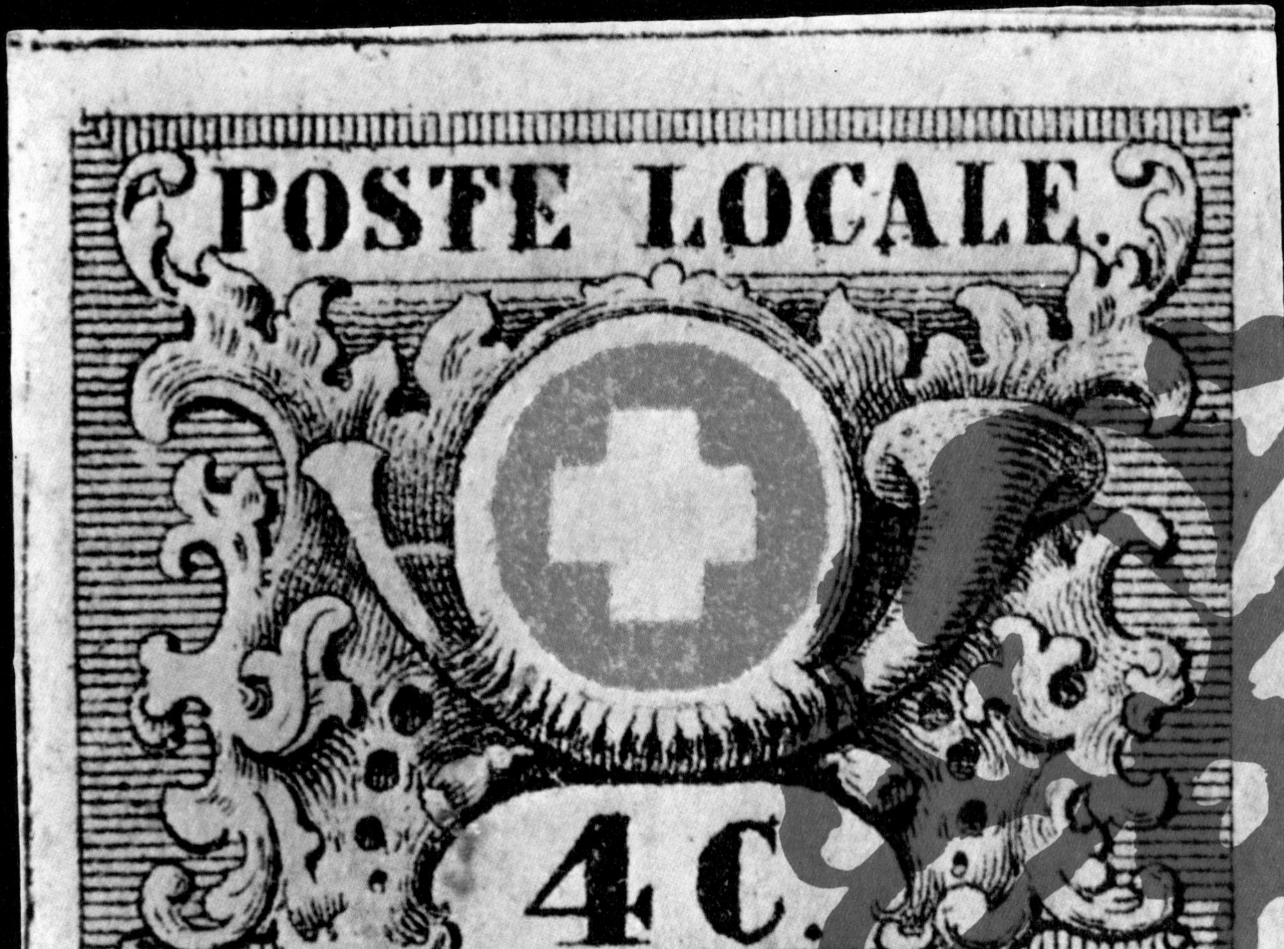
POSTE LOCALE.
4 C.

143, 144 Newfoundland: 1930, the Columbia

mail carried from Newfoundland the then current 75 cents air stamp was overprinted '1933 Gen. Balbo Flight. $4,50'. The colour of the 75 cents was bistre, somewhat similar to the yellow of the 10 cents of the same issue, and either as a trial, or possibly in error, eight examples of the 10 cents were similarly overprinted. Needless to say, they are of extreme rarity.

Balbo's flights to and from the USA were made the occasion of the issue of an extensive series of stamps by Italy. Two special designs were used, consisting of three panels each, and this inevitably resulted in the stamps' being called 'triptyches' [figure 139]. There were two denominations: 5.25 L + 19.72 L and 5.25 L + 44.75 L.

The normal stamps are still relatively common, but much rarer is the higher denomination overprinted with the words 'Servizio di Stato' for use on official mail. Still rarer are the unissued stamps prepared for Balbo's return flight and overprinted 'Volo di Ritorno New York — Roma'. These exist also with the name of the aviator on whose plane the mail was to be carried. One of these items in the Hoffmann sale realized £1,900 and one of the 'Servizio di Stato' triptyches used on a cover flown to Chicago attained £1,700.

Following the success of the *Daily Mail* award for the first transatlantic flight, the Australian Commonwealth government offered a similar prize in 1919 for the first aircraft to fly from England to Australia within thirty days. There was a stipulation that the prize could be won by Australian airmen only. In October of that year, Ross Smith and Keith Smith persuaded Vickers Ltd to enter a machine for this prize, and a plane similar to that used by Alcock and Brown for their transatlantic flight was prepared for the attempt, the main difference being that the Smith plane was equipped with two engines, each of 360 hp.

The machine left Hounslow aerodrome on 12 November 1919, and after making numerous stops on the way, the fliers arrived at Port Darwin, Australia, on 10 December.

From there they proceeded to Cloncurry, and thence to Charleville, in Queensland, where the plane was completely overhauled, and they did not reach Melbourne until 26 February 1920.

They had brought some mail from England and other letters were picked up *en route*. At Melbourne a special vignette was prepared in a design showing the plane in flight above silhouette maps of the British Isles and Australia and bearing the inscription 'First Aerial Post 12 Nov – 10 Dec 1919 England – Australia'. This vignette was printed in deep blue from a half-tone block impressed singly in the centre of a small perforated sheet. Each letter had one of these vignettes minus the margins affixed to it, as well as, in some cases, an Australian postage stamp: an oval cancellation suitably inscribed and dated '26 Feb 1920' was applied to each letter. It is believed that no more than 170 vignettes were produced; 131 were used on letters so that at the most 39 have survived in unused condition. In the Hoffman sale an unused example realized £420.

The world's rarest airmail stamp is the 'Black Honduras'. It is the Honduras 10 cents deep blue postage stamp of 1915-6 surcharged in black 'Aero Correo 25'. Only a single example is now known to exist.

In 1925 the Central American Airline began an airmail service between Puerto Cortés, on the north coast, and Tegucigalpa, the capital of Honduras, since there was no railway between these places. The American owner of the airline, Dr T. C. Pounds, came to an arrangement with the Honduran government for the carriage of mail, whereby, in return for the service, he was to receive the proceeds of a special issue of airmail stamps to be used in addition to normal postage stamps on the flown mail. The Honduran Post Office furnished Dr Pounds with a quantity of regular postage stamps of the 1915-6 issue and gave him permission to supply them with suitable overprints. He arranged a rush job with a printer, whose press was so small that only twelve

145 Australia: the Ross-Smith vignette

of the stamps could be overprinted at a time. Most of the stamps supplied were in sheets of a hundred, so that they had to be divided into blocks of twelve before the overprints could be applied. Different coloured inks were used in the emergency, some stamps being overprinted in red, others in blue, and some in black, and no records were kept of which stamps were overprinted in which colour.

Only four examples have ever been recorded of the twenty-five in black on 10 cents dark blue, but three of them seem to have disappeared mysteriously. The only specimen now known was discovered in June 1930 and subsequently changed hands a few times before being acquired by Thomas A. Matthews. When his collection was sold in New York in 1961, the 'Black Honduras' realized $24,500, at that time a record for an airmail stamp.

In 1919 an experimental flight was made in Colombia from Barranquilla to Puerto Colombia by Knox Martin, an American aeronaut. Two hundred of the then current 2 centavos, carmine, postage stamp were overprinted '1er Servicio Postal Aereo 6 – 18 – 19' for use on mail, and about 160 were so used. The stamps were overprinted in horizontal strips of ten which had been cut from the sheet with a knife, so that the horizontal perforations on most specimens are trimmed to a greater or less extent. The fifth stamp in every strip has an arabic 1 instead of a roman I [figure 149], and only four unused examples of this variety are known to exist; a strip of three with the centre stamp showing the variety was sold for $2,600 at the Hoffman sale.

The world's first stamp used on mail carried by air was issued in the United States of America in 1877. It is called the Buffalo Balloon stamp and it was prepared for balloon flights made by 'Professor' Samuel Archer King. The design is simple but to the point, and shows the balloon 'Buffalo' sailing through the clouds with the figure 5 in a circle on each side; the inscription 'Balloon Postage' appears at the top and 'Five Cents' at the foot.

148 Honduras: 1925 Air 10c

146 (*opposite left*) Togo: 1914 10pf block of four with overprint inverted on upper pair

147 (*opposite right*) German Pos in China: 1900 50pf Tientsin provisional

The stamps were printed in deep blue in sheets of twenty. The press was too small to accommodate a complete sheet at one operation, so the lower ten stamps were printed upside-down in relation to the upper ten, thus causing tête-bêche varieties. A few vertical tête-bêche pairs have survived, one of which realized $1,450 at the Hoffman sale. The same collection contained one of the three known covers flown by King from Gallatin, Tennessee, on 18 June 1877, and addressed to Harrodsburg, Kentucky. This cover, which bears a US 3 cents stamp in addition to the balloon postage, realized $5,250 [figure 140].

In August 1911 the magazine *Scientific American* offered a prize of $50,000 to the first person flying a heavier-

149 Colombia: 1919 airmail in pair showing arabic 1 *(stamp at left)*

than-air machine over the 3,000 miles or so across the United States in either direction, provided that the flight was completed by 10 October. There were five entries, but two withdrew and two others crashed and gave up the attempt. This left only Calbreath Perry Rodgers in the running, and on 17 September he took off from Sheepshead Bay, New York, in a primitive machine, looking much like a box kite, and which he called the 'Vin Fiz'.

After numerous hardships and delays Rodgers eventually reached Long Beach, California, fifty days later, too late to win the prize, but as he said philosophically: 'I've had twice $ 50,000 worth of fun.'

A black 25 cents stamp was produced by the sponsors of the flight, the soft drink manufacturers, the Vin Fiz Company. The design shows a biplane in flight and the inscriptions read 'Rodgers Aerial Post Vin Fiz Flyer'. The stamps were used on souvenir postcards sold to commemorate the flight. Although this stamp, like the Buffalo Balloon issue, must be classed as a semi-official airmail issue, it is one of the rarest items of the United States [figure 134].

An attempt during the late nineteen-twenties to speed up the mails led to the issue of some very rare airmail stamps. In August 1928, on its trip across the Atlantic from New York, the French liner *Ile de France* carried a sea-plane which was to be catapulted with mail when the ship was one day away from the French coast. A fee of 10 francs was charged on every letter, and the French Consul-General in New York authorized the surcharging of the then current 90 centimes and 1 franc 50c French postage stamps with '10 Fr.' and two bars deleting the original denomination [figure 150]. The total number of the 90c surcharged in this way was 2,655; there were 900 of the 1f 50c. The 90c is known with the surcharge inverted. Unused or used on flown covers these provisionals are in great demand; an unused 10 francs on 1f 50c realized £500 at the Hoffman sale.

150 France: 1928 Ile de France 10 francs on 1 franc 50 centimes

ZALA - SOMOGY Steamship Company.
HUNGARY.

n Lake Balaton.

CHAPTER SEVEN

Rare local and telegraph Stamps

THE PHILATELIC DEFINITION of a local is 'a postage stamp of which the franking validity is limited to a town, district, or route'. Locals fall into two groups: government issues and private issues. Private local postage stamps, which at one time were neglected by most collectors, have enjoyed greatly increased popularity since the nineteen-forties, when a new catalogue of them, the first for over forty years, was published.

Some private locals are extreme rarities, and rarity in a local stamp often means that the number of examples known can be counted on the fingers of both hands. Such a degree of rarity in a government-issued postage stamp would mean that its price would be extremely high, but as collectors in general have not yet realized the interest and rarity of certain locals, their price on the market usually fails to reach the height it merits.

One of the world's rarest local issues is that of Gauthier Frères & Cie, a French-based steamship company which operated during 1856-7. This company worked two services under an agreement with the French government, both from Le Havre, one to New York and the other to Rio de Janeiro. The Company had eight ships, five of them previously having been troop transports during the Crimean War. One, the *Barcelone*, began the New York service on 23 February 1856. Three others, the *Cadix*, *Lyonnais* and *Franc Comtois*, operated on the line to Rio de Janeiro.

152 Gauthier Frères: the unique pair of the red stamp

151 (*opposite*) Zala-Samogyi Steamship Company: page from a collection in the USA

For use on mail carried on the South American route the Company issued two stamps, both in the same design, showing a picture of the *Barcelone* and inscribed in the oval framework '*Cie Franco-Americaine. Gauthier Frères & Cie*'. The stamps were undenominated, and one printing was in red, another in blue. The significance of these two colours in relation to the price at which the stamps were sold has not yet been established. When it had been in existence for nearly a year, the Company sustained a serious loss when the *Lyonnais* was sunk after a collision, and 120 lives were lost. Not long afterwards Gauthier Frères & Cie passed out of existence.

The actual date when the stamps were issued and how long they were in use still remains a mystery, but it is a fact that just one blue stamp and six red stamps are known to exist. The unique blue specimen is on a letter addressed to Lisbon; one of the red stamps is also on a letter, addressed to Bordeaux [figure 153]. Both letters are superscribed '*par Franc Comtois*'. Of the other five red examples, two comprise a vertical pair [figure 152] on part of a letter with a similar superscription. These four examples are all in a well-known collection in Illinois, USA. One of the remaining three is in another collection in the USA, and the other two are in English collections. All the stamps bear a monogram cancellation, in black or blue, of the letters 'G. F. & C.' in script. The Tapling collection in the British Museum does not contain this rarity.

The 'Lady McLeod' stamp of Trinidad was the first adhesive postage stamp ever issued in a British colony [figure 132]. Its use was entirely local, and it was issued privately by David Bryce, master of the sixty-ton steamer *Lady McLeod*, for mail carried between Port of Spain and San Fernando.

The stamp was lithographed in blue and was issued about 16 April 1847. Very little is known about the circumstances of its production, but it is believed to have been printed in

An issue of stamps which is comparatively little known

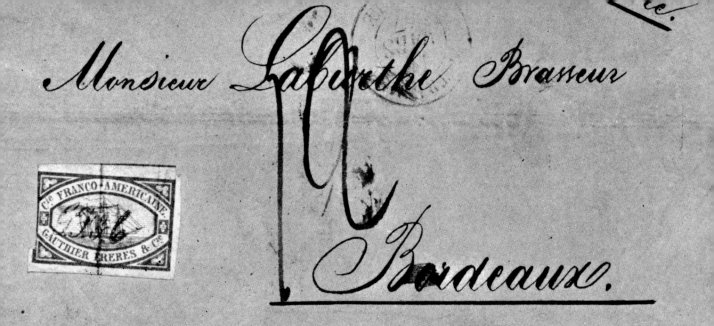

sheets of 100. Where it was printed or by whom has never been discovered.

In use the stamp was cancelled as a rule with a penmark cross, but occasionally a corner would be lifted with the thumbnail and a small piece skinned from the surface of the stamp. In other cases the stamp was left uncancelled. The 'Lady McLeod' is known used on letters, one such item being in the Tapling collection at the British Museum, and perhaps fifty examples, on and off letters, are known altogether.

It is uncertain how long the stamp remained in use. The steamer continued its weekly voyages for two-and-a-half years and it is assumed that the stamp was in use during the whole of the time, but there were no dated postmarks to help solve the mystery of the length of its currency. At one time the 'Lady McLeod' was regarded with disfavour by collectors and one of the early stamp journals went so far as to condemn it as a bogus issue. However, it outlived the obloquy and has shown a rapid increase in value in recent years. A used example in the Caspary collection realized $1,600 in 1956.

153 Gauthier Frères: cover bearing the red stamp

An issue of stamps which is comparatively little known and extremely rare is that of the Zala-Somogyi Steamship Company, which operated a ferry service on Lake Balaton, Hungary, during the eighteen-seventies. This Company was established in 1873 and stamps were issued, probably in 1875, for use on mail carried between Boglár and Fülöprév.

There were three colours of stamps, all in the same design, showing a fouled anchor in a circle enclosed in a rectangular frame, and with the initials of the Company, 'Z.S. G.T.' at the foot. The stamps are imperforate and they were produced by cameo stamping, one at a time. No denomination appears anywhere in the design, and it is thought that the colours red, green and blue denoted different fees or possibly distances over which the mail was carried. In use the stamps were cancelled with an octagonal single-lined mark inscribed with the names Boglár, Fülöprév or Balaton, with the date in the centre, but no year.

It has been estimated that altogether only some twenty-five specimens of these stamps have survived: there are four green stamps, each on a cover, in the Hungarian Postal Museum in Budapest, and the collection in Illinois, already mentioned, contains eight specimens (five green, two red and one blue) [figure 151]; one other example, believed to be in red, was auctioned in Vienna several years after the Second World War. Of the five green examples in the United States, two are used together on part of a parcel delivery note which bears also a Hungarian printed 5 kreuzer stamp, cancelled at Boglár on 16 July 1875. When writing about the stamps in *The Stamp Lover* (Vol. 50, December 1957) Paul F. Rampacher stated that before the First World War he had seen several unused specimens in a nobleman's collection in Hungary. The whereabouts of those stamps are unknown today. The Company did not long continue its postal service and the stamps may have been in use only during 1875.

The Asia Minor Steamship Company operated a mail service between seaports in the Mediterranean, and in about

1868 issued two stamps for use on mail. Both were in the same prosaic design, showing the name of the Company with the value beneath it enclosed in an ornamental oblong frame. Both stamps, the 1 piastre and the 2 piastres, were printed in black on green glazed paper and are imperforate. They were probably in use only a year or two.

So far as can be estimated, somewhere between twenty and thirty examples of the stamps are known to exist, of which ten are in a well-known Turkish collection and five others in the Illinois collection already mentioned; two more are in the Tapling collection at the British Museum. A vertical pair of the 1 piastre is in existence, and the 2 piastres is known used on cover. A cover bearing a 2 piastres stamp realized £650 when sold at auction by Robson Lowe in 1960.

In 1859, three years before the first government issue of Turkey, the Turkish Admiralty Steamship Company issued stamps for use on mail carried by boats operating between ports in the Ottoman Empire. One of these issues, the 'Official' stamp, is very rare [figure 79]. It is printed in claret, is imperforate, and the design shows a steamship sailing to the right and enclosed in an oval frame bearing the inscription '*Ufficio Postale Vapori Ammiragliato*'. Beneath the boat appears the abbreviation 'Po Pe' (*Porto Piastre*). To the right is a space for the denomination to be inserted by hand. The whole design is enclosed in an ornamental rectangular frame. This stamp has been found used on cover.

One of the most curious local issues is that of Sutherland & Co., which operated a stage coach service to and from Yokohama about 1870. The stamps were ¹/₄ boo black on yellow and 1 boo black on rose. The design shows a post rider blowing a horn while mounted on a galloping horse, and the inscriptions show the name of the Company with 'Postage' and the value. Only six examples of the ¹/₄ boo and four of the 1 boo have been recorded, most of them being in Japanese collections [figure 154].

The stamp was first noted and illustrated in the *American*

154 Japan: local issues, Sutherland & Co. ¹/₄ boo

155 Sutherland & Co.: 1 boo altered in manuscript to ¹/₄ boo

156 The stamp of Tiflis

Journal of Philately, 1st series, vol. 5 page 106 (September 1872). Many years afterwards an example of the ¹/₄ boo was acquired by Fred. J. Melville and later passed into a Japanese collection. This remained the only example known until the nineteen-forties, when two other specimens were discovered. Later the existence of the 1 boo was recorded. All but one of the four specimens of the higher value have been altered in manuscript to ¹/₄ boo [figure 155], and it is thought that perhaps the postal rate was reduced and that the higher denomination was little used in its original state. Imitations of both values were made in the nineteen-fifties, but can be recognized immediately because, unlike the originals, they are on thick surface-coloured art paper.

In 1857 a Post Department was established at the Russian town of Tiflis to handle the inter-urban post and a stamp was issued, probably in November, for use on letters. The stamp was embossed in colourless relief on thick white paper and bore the value 6 kopecks; it was imperforate [figure 156]. This rate of 6 kopecks was charged on mail within the town, but letters to Kodshary were charged triple rate.

The stamp was printed in strips of five at the Viceroy's Government Printing Works at Tiflis, and the central design shows the government eagle above the Tiflis arms, with the Russian inscriptions in the frame-work reading 'Tiflis Town Post 6 kop'. The stamp was withdrawn probably in March 1858 and was replaced by issues of the Imperial Post. Fewer than six examples of the Tiflis stamp are known to exist; three were in the collection of Agathon Fabergé which was auctioned by H. R. Harmer in November 1939.

In the days of the Czars the Russian Imperial Post served only the main routes throughout the vast country. People living in more isolated districts were served very poorly, or not at all, by the official postal service. To overcome this difficulty a large number of local councils (*zemstvos*) set up their own rural posts under the authority of an official edict (*ukase*), and issued their own stamps. These present an enormous field for the collector and include some extreme rarities.

Rarest of them all is the bipartite 3 kopecks black on yellow paper issued in 1869 by Kotelnich. This stamp was printed in two parts: at the right was the postage stamp itself with the value on it, and at the left was the counterfoil. In use the stamp portion was cut off and affixed to the letter, while the counterfoil was either handed to the sender or retained by the postal clerk. In the case of this particular issue only one counterfoil has ever been found and the stamp itself is unknown [figure 157].

Sir John Wilson, Keeper of Her Majesty's Philatelic Collections, who has a deep knowledge of *zemstvo* stamps, has said that the world's rarest stamp is generally considered to be the British Guiana 1 cent black on magenta of 1856; but there is an even greater rarity, because, whereas a whole specimen is known to exist of the British Guiana stamp, only half a specimen is known of the Kotelnich issue of 1869.

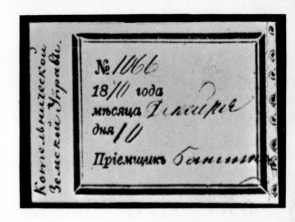

157 The unique half-stamp of Kotelnich 1869, 3 kopecks black on yellow paper

Telegraph Stamps

About the middle of the nineteenth century, and in the days before they were taken over by the British Post Office, numerous private telegraph companies operated in Great Britain. Some of them issued stamps to prepay the fees charged on messages, and among them are six stamps, ranging in value from $4\frac{1}{2}$d to 8s, issued about 1861 by the Submarine Telegraph Company. The stamps are listed in Stanley Gibbons's catalogue for 1940, and also in Walter Morley's catalogue of telegraph stamps of the world, as having been printed in lilac (or mauve) and perforated; but the authors must admit never having seen examples in that state, although proofs in black on card are met with occasionally.

The Post Office took over the private telegraph companies in February 1870 and between then and 1876 no special adhesive stamps were used on telegrams. In 1876, however, the first Post Office Telegraph stamps made their appearance. The initial values were 1d, 3d, 1s and 5s. They were succeeded by other denominations ranging between ¹/₂d and £5 in the course of the next five years.

These stamps were in designs with a portrait of Queen Victoria as the central feature, and in common with the postage stamps current at that time each stamp was inscribed with the number of the printing plate. All the stamps were on watermarked paper and at various times the watermarks consisted of a Shamrock, a Spray of Rose, a Garter, a Crown, a Cross, and an Anchor. The combination of certain plate numbers with certain watermarks has given rise to some great rarities [figure 24].

One of them is the 3s slate-blue (this value was printed only from plate 1) on paper watermarked with a Crown. Very few examples of this stamp are known to exist, either used or unused. The 5s rose on bluish paper with the Anchor watermark is very rare unused, but even rarer is the £5 orange in the same condition, although used examples of the highest value are relatively common. The 5s rose printed from plate 3 on paper watermarked with a Cross exists perforated 12¹/₂ and also 15 x 15¹/₂; the only known example of the 5s with perforation 12¹/₂ is in the Royal Collection, and the same collection includes one of the two known examples of the 3d rose, plate 4, on paper watermarked Spray of Rose. No examples have ever been found of the 1d red-brown, plates 4 or 5, the 3d rose plate 5 watermarked Spray of Rose, the 4d plate 2, and 1s green plate 11 or 12 watermarked Spray of Rose, or the 1s brown-orange plate 11 with the same watermark.

Among other unique telegraph stamps is one in the issue made by the Netherlands in 1877. A solitary example of the 1 cent has been found with the value inverted.

The Russian 20 kopecks telegraph stamp of 1866, perforated 12 [figure 142], is a rarity, but should not be confused with the imperforate reprints with were made years later.

142 *(opposite)* Russia: telegraph stamps, 1886 20 kopecks

The World's rarest and most valuable Issues

This list has been made in one alphabetical sequence under each of two main and two subsidiary headings:

I. GENERAL ISSUES
  (a) Normal stamps
  (b) Varieties

II. LOCAL ISSUES
  (a) Postmasters' stamps
  (b) Private and other issues

The lists have been compiled on the basis of the general collector, not the specialist; that is to say, many exceedingly rare stamps differ from the normal by some more or less small variation in design, perforation or roulette, overprint or paper; for example, New Zealand 1862 3d on pelure paper, Switzerland 1850-1 5r with framed cross, and Austria 1850 1 kr with Tokay roulette, to mention but three. Other stamps are rare in multiples or on cover, or with certain cancellations. The authors have thought it undesirable to burden the lists with such varieties.

The price given after each stamp is the price quoted in *Stanley Gibbons Priced Postage Stamp Catalogue* (1967 edition) and *Scott's Standard Postage Stamp Catalogue* (1967). Where a dash appears in parentheses it denotes that the stamp is either unpriced or not listed in the catalogues. No stamp of an estimated or actual catalogue value lower than $750 has been included.

I. GENERAL ISSUES

(a) *Normal Stamps*

AUSTRIA Newspaper stamps 1851-56 (6kr) red £4,000/ $13,500 (unused)

AUSTRIA Newspaper stamps 1851-56 (30kr) rose £2,000/ $7,500 (unused)

AUSTRIAN ITALY Imperial Journal stamps 1858-59 4kr red (unused) £3,000/$8,000

BAVARIA Postage due 1895 2 on 3pf grey £1,000/(–)

BRITISH GUIANA 1850-51 2c black on *rose* £6,000/$30,000

BRITISH GUIANA 1850-51 4c black on *lemon-yellow* (unused) £2,200 /(–)

BRITISH GUIANA 1850-51 8c black on *green* (unused) £1,250/(–)

BRITISH GUIANA 1852 1c black on *magenta* (unused) £800/$2,500

BRITISH GUIANA 1852 4c black on *deep blue* (unused) £900/$3,250

BRITISH GUIANA 1856 1c black on *magenta* (–)/(–)

BRITISH GUIANA 1856 4c black on *magenta* (used) £750/ $2,250

BRITISH GUIANA 1856 4c black on *blue* £2,000/$8,500

CANADA 1851 12d black (unused) £3,500/$12,500

CEYLON 1857-59 4d dull rose (unused) £4,500/$9,000

CEYLON 1857-59 9d purple-brown (unused) £1,000/$2,850

CEYLON 1912-25 1,000r purple on *red* £3,500/$3,000

GOLD COAST 1883 1d on 4d magenta (–)/(–)

GREAT BRITAIN Official stamps, Board of Education 1902-04 1s green and *carmine* (unused) £2,000/$7,000

GREAT BRITAIN Official stamps, IR Official 1904 6d purple £3,500/$12,000

GREAT BRITAIN Official stamps, IR Official 1904 10s ultramarine £2,500/$6,000

GUADELOUPE Postage Due 1876-9 40c black on *blue* £1,500/$4,000

HAWAII 1851 2c blue £6,000/$22,500

HAWAII 1851 5c blue £1,500/$4,500

HAWAII 1851 13c blue £900/$3000

HAWAII 1851 'H.I. & U.S. Postage' 13c blue £1,750/$5,500

HONDURAS Air 1925 25c in black on 10c deep blue £10,000/$30,000

INDIA, SCINDE 1852 1/2 a scarlet (unused) (–)/(–)

ITALIAN AUSTRIA VENEZIA GIULIA (TRIESTE) 1918 (Nov 3) 10kr deep violet overprinted 'Regno d'Italia/ Venezia Giulia/3.XI.18.' £1,800/$1,500

ITALIAN POS IN CHINA PEKING 1917 (Sept.-Nov.) 40c in black on 11 brown and green (unused) £1,200/$5,000

ITALIAN POS IN CHINA PEKING Postage Due 1918 (July) 4c in black on 10c magenta and orange £1,500/ $3,000

ITALIAN SOMALILAND PARCEL POST 1940 11 lilac (–)/(–)

JOHORE 1926 500 dol blue and red £2,750/$6,000

KENYA, UGANDA AND TANGANYIKA 1912-22 500r green and red on *green* £2,000/$4,250

KENYA, UGANDA AND TANGANYIKA 1922 £25 black and red £2,500/$4,500

KENYA, UGANDA AND TANGANYIKA 1922 £50 black and brown £3,500/(–)

KENYA, UGANDA AND TANGANYIKA 1925-27 £75 purple and grey £8,500/(–)

KENYA, UGANDA AND TANGANYIKA 1925-27 £100 red and black £10,000/(–)

LIBYA Parcel Post stamps 1927-39 5c brown (–)/(–)

MAURITIUS 1847 1d orange-red (unused) £14,000/$42,500 (used) £10,000/$32,500

MAURITIUS 1847 2d blue (unused) £14,000/$42,500 (used) £10,000/$32,500

MAURITIUS 1848 1d orange (unused) £2,250/$6,000

MAURITIUS 1848 2d blue (unused) £2,500/$6,500

MAURITIUS 1859 (Oct.) 2d deep blue (unused) £900/$3,200

MODENA 1859 (Oct. 15) 80c buff (used) £1,250/$3,500

MODENA 1859 (Oct. 15) 80c orange-brown (used) £1,300/$3,500

MOLDAVIA 1858 (July 15) 27p black on *rose* (unused) £2,000/$5,500

MOLDAVIA 1858 (July 15) 81p blue on *blue* (unused) £1,800/$4,500

MOLDAVIA 1858 (July 15) 108p blue on *pink* (unused) £1,000/$3,000

MOLDAVIA 1858 (Nov. 1) 5p black (unused) £1,250/$5,000

MOLDAVIA 1858 (Nov. 1) 80p red (unused) £1,000/$3,000

NAPLES 1860 (Nov.) 1/2 t blue (unused) £4,000/$8,500

NAPLES 1860 (Dec.) 1/2 t pale blue (unused) £1,250/$3,000

NATAL 1902-3 £10 green and orange (unused) £1,600/$3,750

NATAL 1902-3 £20 red and green (unused) £5,000/$12,000

NEW BRUNSWICK 1851 (Sept.) 1s mauve (unused) £1,400/$1,800

NEWFOUNDLAND 1857 (Jan. 1) 1s vermilion (unused) £1,400/$2,250

NEWFOUNDLAND Air 1919 (April 12) 'Hawker' 3c brown overprinted FIRST / TRANS- / ATLANTIC / AIR POST / April, 1919 £1,850/$3,000

NEWFOUNDLAND 1919 (April) 'Morgan-Raynham' 3c brown overprinted in manuscript 'Aerial Atlantic Mail. J.A.R.' £3,500/(–)

NEWFOUNDLAND Air 1927 (May 18) 'De Pinedo' 60c black overprinted in red 'Air Mail / DE PINEDO / 1927' £4,000/$10,000

NIGER COAST PROTECTORATE 1893 (Dec.) 20s in black on 1s green £4,000/$10,000

NIGER COAST PROTECTORATE 1893 (Dec.) 20s in vermilion on 1s green £4,000/$9,000

NIGER COAST PROTECTORATE 1893 (Dec.) 20s in violet on 1s green £4,500/$10,000

NORTHERN NIGERIA 1904 (April) £25 green and carmine £6,000/$15,000

NOVA SCOTIA 1851 1s violet (unused) £1,500/$1,800

PARMA Newspaper stamps 9c black on *blue* (used) £1,500/$4,750

REUNION 1852 15c black on *bluish* (unused) £1,000/$3,000

REUNION 1852 30c black on *bluish* (unused) £1,000/$3,000

SAMOA 1914 (Sep. 3) '1 shilling' on 1m carmine (unused) £1,500/$4,000

SPAIN 1851 (Jan. 1) 2r red (unused) £1,100/$3,000

STRAITS SETTLEMENTS 1906-11 500 dol purple and orange £10,000/(–)

STRAITS SETTLEMENTS 1912-22 500 dol purple and orange-brown £2,000/$3,500

SWITZERLAND, GENEVA 1843 5 + 5c black on *green* £1,850/$8,000

SWITZERLAND, GENEVA 1849 4c black and red £1,350/$3,500

TAHITI 1893 (Aug. 27) 25c ochre, overprinted '1893/TAHITI' (unused) £1,200/$3,000

TOGO BRITISH ISSUES 1914 (Oct. 1) 50pf black and purple on *buff* £1,800/$5,500

TOGO BRITISH ISSUES 1915 (Jan. 7) 50pf black and purple on *buff* £2,500/$4,000

TOGO BRITISH ISSUES 1914 (Oct. 1) 1m carmine (unused) £750/$2,800

TOGO BRITISH ISSUES 1914 (Oct.) 2m blue (unused) £1,200/$4,000

TOGO BRITISH ISSUES 1914 (Oct.) 3m violet-black (–)/(–)

TOGO BRITISH ISSUES 1914 (Oct.) 5m lake and black (–)/(–)

TOGO FRENCH ISSUES 1915 (Jan.) 50pf black and purple on *buff* (unused) £1,500/$4,500

TOGO FRENCH ISSUES 1915 (Jan.) 1m carmine (–)/(–)

TOGO FRENCH ISSUES 1915 (Jan.) 2m blue £3,000/$8,000

TOGO FRENCH ISSUES 1915 (Jan.) 3m violet-black $3,000/(–)

TOGO FRENCH ISSUES 1915 (Jan.) 5m carmine and black (–)/(–)

TUSCANY 1851 2s brick-red on *azure* (unused) £900/$3,250

TUSCANY 1852 60c brick-red on *azure* (unused) £1,500/$4,750

TUSCANY 1860 (Jan. 1) 3l yellow-buff £1,600/$5,500

(b) *Varieties*

ARGENTINA 1862 (Jan. 11) 15c blue, tête-bêche pair £2,000/$5,500

AUSTRIA 1863 2kr yellow, tête-bêche pair (£5,000/(–)

AUSTRIA 1867 3kr red, error of colour £2,750/$8,000

BADEN 1851 9kr black on *green*, error of colour £7,500/$27,500

BARBADOS 1861-70 ?1863 1s blue, error of colour £850/$3,000

BAVARIA 1849 1kr black, tête-bêche pair £3,000/$15,000

BELGIUM 1920 65c black and claret, with centre inverted £800/$2,250

BRAZIL 1843 30c black se-tenant with 60c black (–)/$18,500

BRITISH GUIANA 1850-51 12c blue, with '1' of '12' omitted £2,500/(–)

BUENOS AYRES 1859 (Jan.) 1p deep blue, tête-bêche pair £1,700/$4,750

CAMEROONS (BRITISH OCCUPATION) 1915 3s on 3m surcharge double and 's' inverted (–)/(–)

CAPE OF GOOD HOPE 1855-58 4d black, watermarked (–)/(–)

CAPE OF GOOD HOPE 1861 1d blue, error of colour, £1,400/$4,250

CAPE OF GOOD HOPE 1861 4d vermilion, error of colour £1,850/(–)

CAPE OF GOOD HOPE 1861 4d blue; semi-tête-bêche pair (–)/(–)

CHILE 1911 15c black and purple, with centre inverted £ 800/$ 2,250

DOMINICA 1886 1d on 6d green £ 1,500/$ 3,650

FINLAND 1856 5kop blue, tête-bêche pair £ 1,000/$ 3,000

FINLAND 1856 10kop rose, tête-bêche pair £ 1,200/$ 3,500

FINLAND 1866 5pen brown on *lilac*, tête-bêche pair £ 1,500/$ 4,000

FINLAND 1866 20pen blue on *blue*, with impression of 40pen on back £ 850/$ 3,000

FRANCE 1849 10c bistre, tête-bêche pair (unused) £ 2,500/$ 5,000

FRANCE 1849 15c green, tête-bêche pair £ 5,750/$ 30,000

FRANCE 1849 25c blue, tête-bêche pair (unused) £ 4,750/$ 10,000

FRANCE 1849 1fr orange, tête-bêche pair £ 7,500/$ 20,000

FRANCE 1849 1fr vermilion ('Vervelle') tête-bêche pair (–)/(–)

FRANCE 1853 80c carmine, tête-bêche pair (unused) £ 9,000 $ 22,500

FRANCE 1853 80c rose, with impression of the 1fr on the back (–)/(–)

FRANCE 1853 80c rose, with double impression of the whole design (–)/(–)

FRANCE 1853 1fr carmine, tête-bêche pair £ 2,550/$ 7,000

FRANCE 1869 5fr lilac-grey, with value omitted £ 2,500/$ 7,000

FRENCH COLONIES General Issues 1871-6 10c bistre, tête-bêche pair £ 1,250/$ 3,500

FRENCH COLONIES General Issues 1871-6 20c blue, tête-bêche pair £ 750/$ 2,000

FRENCH POS IN CHINA, CANTON 1903-04 75c brown on *orange*, with name in label inverted £ 3,250/$ 6,500 (NOTE: The same error occurs on stamps overprinted for PAK-HOI and YUNNAN-FOU)

GERMAN COLONIES, KIAUTSCHOU 1900 5 on 5pf on 10pf carmine £ 1,000/$ 2,250

GERMAN POS IN CHINA, TIENTSIN 1900 50pf black and purple on buff (unused) £ 900/$ 4,500

GREAT BRITAIN 1858-64 1d rose red, Plate No. 77 (unused) £ 3,000/$ 10,000 (used) £ 2,000/$ 6,500

GREAT BRITAIN 1860 1½d rosy mauve, error OP-PC, perf (–)/(–)

GREAT BRITAIN 1862 9d straw on *azure* (–)/(–)

GREAT BRITAIN 1867 10d red-brown, watermark Emblems £ 1,500/$ 4,500

GREAT BRITAIN 1869 6d mauve, Plate 10 £ 1,200/$ 4,500

GREAT BRITAIN 1874 4d vermilion, Plate 16 £ 1,500/$ 4,750

GREAT BRITAIN 1876 1s green, Plate 14 £ 1,250/$ 4,500

GREAT BRITAIN 1961 Post Office Savings Bank 2½d with black printing omitted (–)/(–)

GREAT BRITAIN Official stamps Army Official 1902 1d scarlet, with 'Army' omitted (–)/(–)

GREECE 1861 10lep orange on *blue*, with '10' on back

inverted (unused) £ 1,600/(–)

HUNGARY Journal Tax Stamps 1868 1kr blue, pair with one stamp sideways (–)/(–)

INDIA 1854 4as blue and red, with head inverted £ 1,400/$ 7,500

JAMAICA 1919-21 1s orange, with frame inverted (unused) £ 1,000/$ 2,500

JAPAN 1874 20sen purple, syllabic 1 £ 1,250/$ 5,000

KENYA, UGANDA AND TANGANYIKA 1954 5c black and deep brown, with vignette inverted (–)/(–)

LAGOS 1893 ½d on 2d blue and mauve (–)/(–)

MEXICO 1921 10c sepia and blue, with centre inverted (–)/(–)

MOLDAVIA 1858 (July 15) 27par black on *rose*, tête-bêche pair £ 4,250/$ 13,500

MOLDAVIA 1858 (Nov. 1) 5p black, tête-bêche pair (unused) £ 3,000/(–)

MOLDAVIA 1858 (Nov. 1) 80p red, tête-bêche pair £ 1,750/(–)

NEAPOLITAN PROVINCES 1861 ½t black, error of colour £ 1,000/$ 6,000

NEAPOLITAN PROVINCES 1861 2t black, error of colour £ 1,500/$ 6,000

NEWFOUNDLAND Air Balbo 1933 4dol 50c on 10c yellow error (–)/(–)

NEW SOUTH WALES 1850 2d ultramarine (Plate 3) tête-bêche pair (–)/(–)

NEW ZEALAND 1902-09 4d deep blue and brown with centre inverted (–)/(–)

NIGER COAST PROTECTORATE 1893 (Dec.) 20s in violet on 1s green, with surcharge inverted (–)/(–)

NOSSI – BÉ Postage Due 1891 (Oct.) 'o.25' on 20c red on *green*, error £ 1,200/$ 3,000

PARMA 1852 15c grey-black on *dull rose*, tête-bêche pair (–)/(–)

PERSIA 1875 2sh blue, tête-bêche pair (unused) £ 2,000/(–)

PERSIA 1876 1kr carmine, tête-bêche pair £ 2,000/$ 4,500

PERSIA 1876 4kr yellow, tête-bêche pair £ 1,500/$ 4,000

PORTUGUESE GUINEA 1881 40r blue, with error 'Mocambique' (unused) £ 800/$ 3,000

RUSSIA 1875-82 7kop carmine and grey, with centre inverted £ 3,000/$ 2,750

RUSSIA 1902-04 35kop green and lilac, with centre inverted £ 3,000/$ 4,000

SICILY 1859 ½gr cobalt, error of colour (–)/(–)

SPAIN 1851 2r blue, error of colour £ 9,000/$ 32,500

SPAIN 1851 5r chocolate-brown, error of colour £ 800/$ 3,000

SPAIN 1865 12c rose and blue, with frame inverted (unused) £ 1,250/$ 5,000

SPAIN 1867 10m brown, tête-bêche pair (unused) £ 2,000/$ 7,000

SPAIN 1867 25m rose and blue, with centre inverted £ 2,000/$ 7,000

SWEDEN 1855-57 3sk-bco yellow, error of colour (–)/(–)

SWITZERLAND 1882-98 5c marone, tête-bêche pair £1,100/

TOGO BRITISH ISSUES 1914 (Oct. 1) 10pf carmine, overprint tête-bêche in vertical pair £750/(–)

TOGO BRITISH ISSUES 1914 (Oct.) 25pf black and red on *yellow* error 'TOG' £2,500/$7,500

TOGO BRITISH ISSUES 1914 (Oct. 1) 2m blue, with overprint inverted (unused) £1,000/$3,750

TRANSVAAL 1869 1s deep green, tête-bêche pair £1,000/ $3,000

[NOTE: This stamp exemplifies numerous rare tête-bêche varieties in the early stamps of Transvaal. For further details see *Transvaal Postage Stamps* by J. H. Curle and A. E. Basden (London, 1940)]

USA 1869 15c blue and brown, with centre inverted £800/ $3,250

USA 1869 24c purple and green, with centre inverted (unused £3,000/(–)

USA 1869 30c ultramarine and lake, with flags inverted £1,600/$7,000

USA 1901 2c black and carmine-red, with centre inverted £1,250/$4,000

USA Air 1918 24c blue und carmine, with centre inverted (unused) £4,500/$18,500

URUGUAY 1858 120c blue, tête-bêche pair (unused) £2,000/$5,750

URUGUAY 1858 180c green, tête-bêche pair £2,000/ $5,750

URUGUAY 1858 180c dull red, error of colour (–)/(–)

VIRGIN ISLANDS 1867-8 1s crimson, with centre omitted £1,400/$4,500

WESTERN AUSTRALIA 1854 4d blue, with frame inverted £1,600/$6,000

II. LOCAL ISSUES

(a) *Postmasters' Stamps*

BERMUDA, PEROT ISSUES 1848-56 1d black £3,750/ $25,000

BERMUDA, PEROT ISSUES 1848-56 1d red £4,500/ $25,000

BERMUDA, PEROT ISSUES 1861 (?) 1d red £1,750/(–)

BERMUDA, THIES ISSUE 1860 1d £4,250/(–)

CANADA New Carlisle 1851 3d black (–)/(–)

MEXICO, CHIAPAS 1867 8r black or rose £1,200/$2,500

MEXICO, TLACOTALPAN 1856 ½r black £800/$4,000

USA Alexandria 1846 5c black on *bluish* £6,000/$25,000

USA Alexandria 1846 5c black on *buff* £3,000/$9,000

USA Annapolis 1846 5c carmine-red £5,250/$18,500

USA Baltimore 1846 10c black on *white* £4,000/$15,000

USA Baltimore 1846 10c black on *bluish* £5,000/$17,000

USA Boscawen 1846 5c blue £2,750/(–)

USA Lockport 1846 5c red £3,000/$12,500

USA Millbury 1846 5c black on *azure* £2,500/$9,000

USA St Louis 1845-6 5c se-tenant with 10c (–)/(–)

USA St Louis 1845 20c black on *grey* £1,200/$4,750

USA St Louis 1845-6 20c black on *greenish* £2,000/$7,500

USA CONFEDERATE STATES Grove Hill 1861 5c black £3,000/$9,000

USA CONFEDERATE STATES Mount Lebanon 1861 5c red-brown (–)/$10,000

USA CONFEDERATE STATES New Smyrna 1861 5c black £1,275/(–)

USA CONFEDERATE STATES New Smyrna 1861 10 on 5c black £1,500/$4,000

USA CONFEDERATE STATES Unionville 1861 5c black on *bluish* £900/$3,000

II. LOCAL ISSUES

(b) *Private and other issues*

GAUTHIER FRÈRES 1857 undenominated blue (–)/(–)

GAUTHIER FRÈRES 1857 undenominated red (–)/(–)

JAPAN Sutherland & Co. ¼ boo black on *yellow* (–)/(–)

JAPAN Sutherland & Co. 1 boo black on *rose* (–)/(–)

RUSSIA ZEMSTVO ISSUES Kotelnich 1869 3kop black on *yellow* (–)/(–)

[NOTE: Of many Zemstvo stamps only single examples are known, and fewer than six exist of many others. For details see *Die Postwertzeichen der Russischen Landschaftsaemter* by C. Schmidt and A. Fabergé (St Petersburg, 1908-15), and *Sammlung Russischer Landschaftsmarken im Reichspostmuseum* by C. Schmidt Berlin, 1934)]

RUSSIA Tiflis 1857 6kop white (embossed) (–)/(–)

SWITZERLAND Rigi Staffel undenominated, red (–)/(–)

SWITZERLAND Rigi Staffel undenominated, violet (–)/(–)

TRINIDAD 1847 (April 24) 5c blue (unused) £1,200/(–)

USA Carriers Charleston, South Carolina, Beekman's City Post 1860 2c black on *bluish* (–)/(–)

USA Carriers Charleston, South Carolina, Martin's City Post 1858 2c black on bluish (–)/$2,000

USA City Despatch, New York City, 1846 2c red (–)/(–)

USA Clarke's Circular Express, NYC, 1863-5 (1c) blue (–)/(–)

[NOTE: These are typical of rare US local stamps. Of many other local issues in the USA only single examples are known, and fewer than six exist of many others. For further details see *The Local Posts of the United States*, by Dr D. S. Patton (Robson Lowe Ltd, 1967)]